Easy
Edibles

Easy Edibles

by
Sheri Repucci

A Beginner's Guide
to Growing Organic Food
in the Lower Great Lakes Region

Alice Greene & Co.
ANN ARBOR

Published by
Alice Greene & Co.
219 South Main Sreet, Suite 203
Ann Arbor, MI 48104

ISBN 978-1-935770-00-8

13   12   11   10

08   07   06   05

SUSTAINABLE Certified Fiber
FORESTRY   Sourcing
INITIATIVE
Label applies to the text stock www.sfiprogram.org

www.alicegreene.com

This book is dedicated to my father, Lorenzo Repucci, who taught me not only how to chase rabbits from my garden with sheer unabashed abandon, but also how to find joy and laughter in the smallest of life's moments.

His contagious thirst for life had no bounds when he was tending to his garden, his wife, or to his children. May his spirit, sprinkled throughout this book, rub off on all who read it.

Contents

To the New Gardener

Gardens are wonderful places that can easily draw us in: they feed us, they entertain us, and they provide us with exercise and fresh air. However, gardening's real appeal is that it enlivens us in ways that few other activities can. In our world, we have few places we can go and simply be, where our unique ideas of beauty, our individual taste in food, our personal ways of connecting with nature, and our own sense of passing time can be expressed without judgment or compromise. To this end, I offer this book and this thought: make your garden your own and you will be rewarded with the pleasures of a lifetime. Strive always to make it your own—make it fill your senses, satisfy your emotions, and comfort you physically.

As a new gardener it may not be obvious at first how to go about making a garden satisfy you on so many levels, but as the seasons pass, ideas will come to you in subtle, if not obvious ways. You may find yourself creating a place to sit and relax; you may place a small statue or garden ornament in among the plants; your straight rows might start to curve ever so slighty or they might take on a meandering feel, with paths that curve and twist around each crop rather than squared segments evenly spaced. You even might find the color of the plants you choose changes over time to satisfy your personal color preference. The options for how to make the garden your own are endless, guided only by what you need to feel comfortable and joyous while working or dwelling in your garden space.

This book is designed so that you can learn about gardening step by step, or skip around from chapter to chapter, as you desire.

Chapter 1 shares my enthusiasm for gardening in the lower Great Lakes region and lets you know what makes gardening in this region special.

Chapter 2 presents key concepts crucial to the art of organic gardening: the location of your plantings, the vitality of your soil, your choice of plants, and knowing what takes time and energy in the garden throughout the growing season.

Chapter 3 shows you the steps of gardening organically, including improving your soil, planting and supporting, and composting.

Chapters 4 and 5 are reference sections outlining the basics of common and easy-to-grow vegetables, herbs and edible flowers. These chapters also provide journal space to record your experiences with each plant.

Chapter 6 goes straight to the heart of growing edibles: providing nourishing and delicious food for the table. Here you will find everything you need to know to clean, store, cook, and preserve your bounty. You'll also find simple, delicious recipes that take full advantage of your harvest. Of course, the information in this chapter is also of use for any vegetable you buy at your local farmer's market or grocery store.

Chapter 7 is a final reference section, a listing of vegetables that have a history of causing untold frustration in the lives of new gardeners. You'll find out why some plants can be difficult to grow, and why gardeners love to grow them in spite of their challenges.

No matter in which order you choose to read this book, keep in mind: plants don't read. They are odd beasts that, I swear, sometimes grow in ways opposite to what we expect just to confuse us. Don't worry too much if your plants are not doing exactly what you had imagined. And finally, if you're not interested in gardening in the ways that others are, concentrate on finding your own best way in the garden, making it truly your own. May it fill your senses, excite your emotions, and stock your kitchen with good food.

Chapter 1
Gardening in the Lower Great Lakes

Food is a deeply personal matter, influenced by our cultural backgrounds, our individual tastes for flavor, smell and color, and our budgets. While the typical grocery store sells a limited selection of vegetables, growing your own vegetables gives you almost unbounded opportunities to experiment with different foods, allowing you to find ones that fully satisfy your tastes while treating your wallet gently. Growing vegetables that mesh more closely with personal tastes is one of the most compelling reasons gardeners continue to garden year after year.

As if choice and cost were not reasons enough to grow your own food, there are many who swear homegrown and freshly picked vegetables and fruit have an intensity of flavor unmatched by anything purchased in a grocery store. While not quite sure how to define it, I do admit there is something deeply satisfying about biting into a vegetable or piece of fresh fruit while the sun's warmth is still clinging to it.

Growing your own food here in the lower Great Lakes also connects you with the area's long history as a farming region. The soil and climate are so perfect for growing vegetables that this region holds claim to being one of the top three producers in the United States of beans, cabbage, celery, corn, cucumbers, and squash, to name a just a few.

The Lower Great Lakes Region

The lower Great Lakes region covers a vast area defined by four of the five Great Lakes: Michigan, Huron, Erie and Ontario. This region includes the southern portions of Michigan, Wisconsin and Ontario, northern portions of Illinois, Indiana, Ohio, and Pennsylvania, and western portions of New York. Covering considerable stretches of rural areas, the lower Great Lakes region also contains large urban areas, including Milwaukee, Chicago, Gary, Grand Rapids, Detroit, Toledo, Cleveland, Buffalo, Windsor and Toronto.

The weather in this region is characterized by the moisture it receives throughout the year, providing hot and humid summers as well as snow-covered, chilly winters. The large bodies of water that define the Great Lakes have a moderating effect on the bitterly cold winter temperatures that blow from the north, producing the "lake-effect snow" that so heavily blankets portions of this region.

Climate and the Growing Season

The temperature contrast from summer to winter in this region offers a challenging environment, but it also offers distinct advantages for gardeners. The cold weather helps keep the insects at bay and suppresses the intensity of viruses and molds that can plague warmer climates. The deep snow that covers this region provides a hidden gift to the gardener: not only does snow cover help insulate the roots of perennial plants, but each time snow falls through the atmosphere it picks up minute quantities of nitrogen. As the piles of snow melt in the spring the soil receives a small infusion of nitrogen, providing vegetable and landscape plantings with an early burst of fertilizer.

Soils

Gardening organically in this region brings both great joys, as we strive to work with Mother Nature rather than fighting her, and interesting challenges, as nature occasionally fights back. The soils that are found in the region vary from clay to sand, which can be maddening if you live in an area on one extreme of that spectrum. But, take heart, soils are amendable! We can add organic matter and greensand (a mix of sand and glauconite, a sedimentary deposit that provides micronutrients) to clay, making it easier to work and better at draining off water. Likewise, we can add organic matter to sand to help retain water and add nutrients.

Trends in Gardening

Heirlooms

Heirloom vegetables—eating them, growing them, and propagating their seeds—is a relatively new trend among organic gardeners. While there is not a clear consensus on the definition of an heirloom, they are generally considered to be plant varieties that were popular and available many generations ago that reproduce by open-pollination.

Heirloom vegetables are sought after for their unusual flavors and their wide variety of colors and shapes. In the United States, for example, there are only about ten varieties of potatoes available from the grocery stores. By contrast, in Bolivia where potatoes originated, there are over a thousand varieties to choose from, many of which we can grow in our own gardens here in the lower Great Lakes region. One exotic example is the Purple Peruvian, a fingerling-shaped potato with a deep purple color on both the inside flesh and its outer skin. It makes a dramatic display on the dinner plate.

Heirloom tomatoes are also highly sought after for their delicious, satisfying flavors. One popular tomato variety is the Cherokee Purple, a large beefsteak with an intensely spicy, smoky flavor. This tomato, which ripens to a dark brown-black color, was cultivated by Native American Cherokee tribes from the Tennessee area.

Urban Gardening

Gardening in unused spaces found in cities is not a new trend; it is as old as the world's oldest cities. However, there is renewed interest in gardening among city dwellers as we try to re-establish healthy eating patterns and to bring food production closer to home. Gardening in a city can take many forms, including planting flowers in small spaces (like window boxes) to help beautify an area. However, the term "urban gardening" typically refers to planting vegetable gardens in the large spaces found between buildings in an urban area. This can mean informally planting in abandoned properties, but it can also mean negotiating with local churches and schools to establish gardens for community use (many have underutilized lawn areas). Most large cities in the lower Great Lakes region, and many of its smaller cities and towns, have well-established community garden programs; others are in the process of creating such shared spaces.

Edible Landscaping

A relatively new trend, edible landscaping is an outgrowth of the movement to reduce the amount of lawn in the urban and suburban landscape. It is a simple concept aimed at replacing lawn and other non-edible landscaping materials with plants that produce fruit, vegetables, or herbs. Examples of edible plants that are finding their way into the landscape are perennial herbs in place of smaller landscaping bushes, basil used as a green edging around annual flower beds, strawberries and wintergreen berries as a ground cover, rainbow chard as a color accent, and, in locations with peat-like soil, blueberry bushes with their fiery fall color.

School Gardening Programs

Created to educate children on the full cycle of food—from seed through harvest to the dinner plate—school garden programs are experiencing a welcome resurgence in the United States. They are an old trend made new again by a fresh infusion of enthusiasm. Alice Waters, a prominent chef, reinvisioned the concept of school gardening and coined the phrase "Edible Schoolyard." She has gone on to become a national advocate for teaching children how to both grow and cook their own food. Her efforts have had a wonderfully energizing effect on school-based garden programs, and there are many vibrant school garden programs in the lower Great Lakes region.

Food Banks: Donating Excess Produce

All gardeners, beginners and experienced alike, occasionally underestimate how fruitful their gardens will be. Zucchini, tomatoes and cucumbers are notorious over-producers, leaving the gardener desperate at times to find neighbors and friends willing to take more. Gardeners, traditionally generous, often donate their excess to local food banks or charities that feed the hungry. A wonderful way to share a big harvest, donating extra crops has, over the years, spurred a new trend: "plant a row for the hungry." The idea is quite straightforward: plant an additional section of your garden with vegetables intended for your local food bank. Note that it is common for a food bank to receive an abundance of the more fruitful vegetables, like tomatoes and zucchini, while taking in few beets, carrots, or greens. If growing vegetables for your local charity appeals to you, it is wise to call them before planting to see what vegetables they need most.

What an Opportunity!

Gardening in the lower Great Lakes region is easy to learn and the variety of crops that you can grow will delight you and fill your kitchen with nutritious food. Our changeable weather provides both the moisture and warmth that make gardening in this region so productive. The traditional gardening techniques described in this book have stood the test of time, providing gardeners throughout this region with bountiful crops of vegetables year after year.

I hope that you will have fun gardening and, with time and experience, will look for new challenges and opportunities.

Chapter 2

Key Concepts for Success

For all gardeners, but especially for those in the lower portion of the Great Lakes, where weather is often fickle and the growing season is relatively short, there are four concepts that can dramatically improve your success and enjoyment of gardening: the location of your plantings, the fertility of your soil, your choice of plants, and your knowledge of what takes time and effort in the garden.

I have helped people of all ages learn to garden organically for more than a dozen years—some have been new to vegetable gardening and others have been experienced gardeners who were new to organic methods. Along the way I have come to believe that success comes most easily when these four concepts are taken into account, both in the planning and the growing of a garden.

What follows in this chapter may make organic gardening seem complicated—I realize that this is a common reaction for new gardeners. Please don't let this discourage you. The information in this book will guide you and help you plan a garden that is just right for you. It will help you get the most out of your garden with the least effort by enlisting nature's help.

Location, Location, Location

Where to plant a garden? Choosing a garden location involves first making decisions about how you want to garden: traditional garden beds, raised beds using built structures for ease of access, or containers. Considering how to maximize your environment will help you decide which style or styles of gardening might be most suitable. Environmental factors include the amount of sunlight a particular location receives, how windy or how still the site is, the availability of water, and the potential for damage from wildlife and everyday life. While the list might seem a bit long, it's designed to encourage you to both explore the opportunities and avoid the obstacles of possible locations.

Traditional Gardening Beds

Traditional gardening beds have many advantages, such as low costs and excellent water retention, and they're one of the quickest ways to start a garden. Simply dig up a section of earth with a shovel or digging fork, turn it over, and break up the soil to reduce large clumps, removing any large stones. Add organic matter such as compost (see page 22), rake the soil flat, and plant seeds or transplants. It's a fast way to get started, though it may give your back a workout!

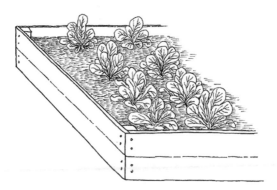

Raised-Bed Gardening

Raised beds are a variation on traditional garden beds. Typically, wooden boards or bricks are used to create a frame structure, which sits on the ground. The structure is then filled with soil. Raised beds are generally about a foot high, but can be made much higher.

Gardeners choose raised beds primarily for three reasons. First, for anyone with a physical disability, a raised bed can provide easier access and be an enormous aid in reducing muscle strain. Second, if your soil is primarily sand or clay, you can simply fill the raised bed with better soil. And finally, raised beds can clearly establish the borders of the garden, which can help to keep rabbits, dogs, children (and stray soccer balls, among other things) out of the garden.

The general growing techniques used in traditional gardening beds (see Chapter 3) are also used in raised-bed gardening. Weeding a raised bed is somewhat easier than a traditional garden bed, as crops are often planted closer together, providing less space for weeds to take hold. But raised gardens are not perfect; where the structure meets the ground is a haven for weeds, and this area can be a bit difficult to keep neat.

Container Gardening

Container gardening, compared to traditional garden beds, is unique unto itself. As with raised beds, using containers allows you to start with good soil. Container gardening can also provide creative solutions to a variety of gardening challenges: tall vessels raise the soil level for those with back problems or other physical disabilities, containers can be placed where there is no available land (for example, on a cement patio, deck, or walkway), and containers can be used as art objects to enhance the environment.

Planting in containers is easy, and weeding, in particular, is rarely a problem. However, containers are not without challenges. Water in garden containers evaporates at a faster rate than in either traditional or raised-bed gardens. Pots made from impervious materials (plastic, metal, glazed ceramic) are the most efficient at retaining water, pots made from clay and wood are the least.

Setting up a watering system (often a drip-line system with an automatic timer) can reduce having to hand-water your containers frequently. If you are away during the hot and often dry summer months found in our region, it is wise to find a willing gardening buddy, neighbor, or friend to water.

The most frequent material used in containers is clay. Oh, how we do seem to love the look of clay pots. However, in the cold of our winters clay often cracks if soil is kept in the pot and the pot is left outside. This is caused by the water in the soil expanding when it freezes, pushing outward on the fragile clay until it gives way. The solutions for avoiding this are emptying the clay pots of soil at the end of each season, or moving the whole pot, soil and all, into a protected space like a garage for the winter. Alternatively, you may wish to exclude clay pots from the garden, using instead wood, metal, plastic, or some of the new materials designed to withstand winter weather.

Sunlight

Sunlight, needless to say, is one aspect of choosing a location that simply can't be underestimated. While most vegetables, herbs and flowers prefer full sun—a minimum of 6 hours of direct sun each day—there are exceptions. Tomatoes for example, thrive nicely in locations where they receive 3 to 4 hours of full sun with the remaining hours receiving dappled light. Parsley and mint can be grown with good results in light shade, especially if they receive at least a few hours of direct sun each day.

Lettuce plants will wilt or burn if they are exposed to full sun during the hottest part of the summer. For this and other crops sensitive to full sun, there is an easy solution: plant them on the north or northwest side of much taller plants like tomatoes, for shading during summer's hottest days.

All new gardeners should become familiar with both the sunlight requirements for the plants they wish to grow (see Chapter 4) and the sunlight patterns in the various locations where they are contemplating situating their gardens.

Locating Gardens Wisely

Other location considerations for planning your first garden include aesthetics, space use, proximity to water, and local wildlife. How well you like the look and feel of your garden will naturally affect how much time and effort you're likely to invest in your garden's success.

Space use is important as well. If you frequently throw large parties in your yard, have active children who use the yard, or have a dog who tears up every patch of ground you own, consider these factors when you decide where to place your garden and what style of garden would work best (hint: raised-bed gardens are great for avoiding dog damage).

Proximity to water and its impact on your success in the garden can not be stressed enough. If you need to carry buckets and buckets of water down to the garden every time the soil dries out, you are likely to find yourself avoiding watering as the summer goes on. If a hose will reach but it cuts across the lawn and has to be wrapped up each time so the lawn mower won't chew it up, or if the sheer weight of that much hose is too heavy for you, then perhaps you need to rethink the location.

Alternatively, you might keep your eyes peeled for an inventive way to get an extension hose to your garden. I once ran across a garden where a hose had been cleverly threaded through PVC piping, which was routed around the lawn. It was impervious to lawn mower damage and out of sight.

Wildlife

Local wildlife. This issue can be a tough one to get around, depending on what wildlife you have roaming near your garden. Defending your garden against deer is a sore subject among even the most experienced gardeners. My only advice is either to plant in containers placed against a wall (you still may have to wrap them with chicken wire), or to build fences. Rabbits are also a painful topic, but they are

more easily managed than deer. Rabbits can't climb, so using raised beds at least 2 feet high can help, as can chicken wire fencing around a traditional garden (you will have to bury the wire under the ground about a foot, as these creatures will happily dig under fences to get to your tasty vegetables). The best advice on defending against wildlife often comes from neighbors and community members who have been gardening in the area for many years—seek out their advice if you are fighting wildlife for your vegetables. Other good resources are your local extension office, extension websites, and your local library.

Soil Fertility

It is said that organic gardeners first grow soil, then plants. That's because they rely on a good understanding of soil structure and the addition of natural materials, rather than on synthetic fertilizers, to provide soil fertility. Soil science may not be a topic enjoyed by the majority of the population (including the gardening population), but, as a beginner gardener, you should know at least the basics.

Soil holds the nutrients and water needed for plant growth, as well as providing a very clever mechanism through which water is either retained or drained off quickly. Additionally, soil is the medium that enables a plant to grab hold and stabilize its footing, allowing it to stand upright to air its leaves and to support the weight of its fruit.

Soil structure refers to the relative mix of large and small granules found in the soil. The soil in the lower Great Lakes region is primarily comprised of two types of particles: sand and clay. Placing a piece of sand next to a piece of clay under a microscope reveals that a particle of clay is quite small relative to a particle of sand. The challenge for gardeners is the proportion of sand particles to clay particles in any given soil, and the effect this has on the growth of plants.

What defines a good soil structure can vary somewhat based on what plant you are trying to grow, but overall, a *loose soil* with an approximately even mix of both sand and clay is ideal. It provides a good balance of water and nutrient retention while providing a good rooting medium for the plants, allowing them to stand upright.

Clay soil has far more clay in it than sand. Few vegetables prefer a heavy clay soil, although many grow in it without apparent problems if watering requirements are watched closely. And finally, a sandy soil has far more sand than clay. Root vegetables love to grow in a sandy, soil structure, as it allows the roots to easily expand.

Water and Nutrient Retention

In clay soil, the particles are so tightly packed that it is difficult for water to flow through the soil easily. As a result, clay holds onto water more efficiently than a sandy or balanced soil. (If you have seen water standing in puddles long after a rain, chances are you were looking at clay soil.)

The compacted nature of this soil has both advantages and disadvantages. Root vegetables grown in clay can suffer from root rot or dampness diseases if they sit too long in water-logged clay soil. In addition, in the heat of the summer when soils dry out between waterings, clay soils tend to become almost rock hard if not watered regularly. Dehydration and compaction problems can occur in this situation, making plants more prone to diseases and pests.

On the other hand, clay soils are very fertile because they hold onto their nutrients extremely well. A new garden plot dug into a clay soil typically doesn't need to have nutrients added in its first few years. It will, however, need organic material, such as compost, added to reduce compaction and improve drainage.

In contrast, sandy soils, with their large particles that form air pockets, allow water to rush right through. Because of this inability to retain water, sandy soils require frequent and consistent watering throughout the growing season. Sandy soils also lack the nutrients found in clay soils, and they must be amended to provide them. The addition of organic material like compost will help with both problems.

Root Penetration and Plants' Footings

In tightly packed clay soils, the roots of large and aggressive plants like tomatoes and squash can push apart the bonds of clay soil and grab hold to anchor themselves. Delicate plants, though, have a hard time anchoring their roots in a tight clay soil. Root vegetables also have a difficult time in tightly packed clay soils; their roots need to easily expand both downward and outward in the soil without spending excess energy doing so. Sandy or loose soils can easily be pushed aside by growing roots, allowing for larger and better-formed vegetables.

Changing Your Soil Structure

While few gardens start out with perfect soil, you can improve soil that has too much clay or too much sand by adding as much organic matter—humus or compost—as possible. Humus typically consists of composted manure, leaf mulch, or peat. Peat and composted cow manure can be purchased from your local gardening center. Leaf mulch can be made from leaves gathered each fall. If possible, add humus to your soil in the fall when the growing season is over. This will allow it time to finish decomposing before planting in the spring.

Compost can be added to your soil at any time. Typically, it is made from yard trimmings and vegetable kitchen scraps that have decomposed until the material has become small particles that are not recognizable in their original form (see page 38). Many cities have compost facilities where they gather and compost yard wastes such as leaves, grass clippings, and tree branches. If you have access to the fresh compost that these facilities generate and often sell back to the public, take advantage of it. The soils that these facilities produce are ideal for growing vegetables.

Choosing Plants: Grow What You Love

As a newcomer to vegetable gardening, you probably have some idea of what you want to grow. Mixed in might be a few ideas of what you think you're supposed to grow. In the lower Great Lakes region and almost everywhere else, gardeners seem to be assaulted with the requirement that a garden just isn't a garden without certain plants, chief among them tomatoes. Ah, baloney—if you don't like tomatoes, don't feel you must grow them. And even if you love tomatoes, with time you'll realize that at the exact moment your tomatoes are ripe all the other tomatoes in the lower Great Lakes are also ripe, and everyone is trying desperately to give away their extras (the same is true for zucchini, summer squash, and cucumbers).

If you find you do not have enough space in your garden for all the vegetables you'd like to grow, you may well choose to eliminate plants like tomatoes to save room for vegetables that are either hard to find or expensive to purchase. If you don't really like a certain vegetable, growing it yourself is not likely to make that change. It can, but it's not terribly likely. So, for your first garden or two, plant vegetables you already know you love. As your gardening experience grows, you will naturally try new and different vegetables.

Consider Culinary Needs and Quantities

Some vegetables, like lettuce, radishes, and spinach, are often eaten straight from the garden. Others require more time for preparation and cooking, or present special challenges. For example, if you love beets but you don't like to contend with their red dye, which can often stain clothing, then by all means, grow the golden variety of beets instead, or leave the space in the garden for something else.

Finally, think about the quantity of individual vegetables you will eat. Lettuce is an excellent crop for first-time gardeners, but just how much lettuce can you actually eat in one week? Would a short row of, say, eight plants work for you versus a long row of thirty that are all ready to pick (and eat) at the same time?

Time Constraints and Ease of Effort

A final important consideration for a successful garden is determining just how much time you have or want to spend working in your garden, and plan accordingly. The time and physical-energy commitments in the garden vary significantly throughout the season and can be intensified by the unpredictable, changeable weather in this region, which can turn from being too wet and cold to too hot and dry, almost instantly.

May through June demands the most time and energy from gardeners in the lower Great Lakes: soil must be prepared and seeds and transplants must be planted. July and August require relatively less time and energy because the plants are established and growing, but there are additional time and energy demands of watering and weeding. In September and October, the pace picks up again with harvesting and year-end cleaning and closing of the garden.

Preparing the Garden: Spring and Fall

Perhaps the most time-consuming and physically demanding of gardening tasks is preparing the garden for planting in the spring and "putting it to bed" at the end of the season. Whether you are preparing the ground for a traditional garden bed or you are growing in raised beds or containers, you will invariably be digging, lifting, amending, or shoveling soil in early spring and again in late fall. If you are gardening in containers, you may also be lifting and moving pots.

Planting

Everyone seems to love this part of gardening; it hardly seems fair to list it among the chores of gardening. Planting involves either sowing seeds or placing *starts* (young plants) into the beds or containers where they will grow. While neither seeds nor transplants are much more time consuming than the other, seeds often require additional effort to label rows or areas to identify what was planted where. This is particularly important if you are planting vegetables close together. Though the biggest time investment for planting is in the spring, there are some vegetables you may want to plant every two weeks throughout the season for a continuous harvest throughout the summer.

Watering

This is perhaps the most time consuming of all the gardening tasks. Typically, it doesn't take a lot of physical energy, but the time commitment is high. In addition, watering must be carried out throughout the entire growing season, with the possible exception of spring, when the lower Great Lakes region is often lucky enough to have adequate rainfall. If you go away during the summer when it's very warm and often too dry, you might consider arranging for a fellow gardener, neighbor, or friend to water for you.

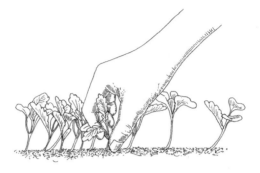

Thinning

Once the seeds you've planted have started to sprout, you're likely to be a bit surprised by how many plants you suddenly have. Even the most experienced gardener often over-plants as a way of ensuring enough plants sprout successfully, especially if the seed packet is old and the viability of the seeds is in question. In addition, there are a few vegetables, including carrots and lettuce, that are sown by "broad-casting" (sprinkling many seeds at once). Thinning, or removing extra plants, is not physically hard, except perhaps for the bending involved; however, thinning does take time.

Weeding

Ah yes, the bane of a gardener's life, weeding. Try as we might and as inventive as we may be, gardeners have yet to find a way around the ongoing need to weed. We have tricks that help postpone the agony—for example, creating barriers from layers of newspapers strewn with loose straw or black plastic—but eventually the weeds will work their way through or around almost everything put in their way, and we are forced into the garden to weed. Weeding takes both time and physical effort, especially in late spring and early summer.

Pruning

Often not talked about as a necessity for the vegetable gardener, pruning can make all the difference in how happy you are with your garden and even how productive your vegetable plants are. Some plants, particularly tomatoes, produce better individual fruit if the plant is pruned regularly, discouraging it from over-fruiting. Pruning will also keep neighboring plants from being shaded, as well as improve the look of your garden.

Disease and Insect Damage

Though organic gardening tends to attract far fewer problems than non-organic methods, it does not provide a guarantee. Employing organic methods to create healthy soil and keeping the garden clean of diseased and weakened plants can, however, reduce your chances of crop damage from disease and insects.

The challenges of disease and insect damage vary during the growing season and from year to year, depending on what virus, mold, or insect population is affecting your area now. For seasonal information on the diseases and insects affecting crops in your state, look up the Crop Reports on your state's or province's agricultural extension website. (See page 143 for a listing of the websites for the lower Great Lakes region.)

How much time and effort you invest in prevention and control often depends on your tolerance for disease and insect damage in the garden. With time, experienced gardeners determine how much of each crop they are willing to lose to natural events before they step in with damage control. The amount of physical effort needed for this is minimal, with the exception of building fences or barriers to prevent damage from wildlife.

Harvesting

Picking and eating produce from the garden is another joy that I hesitate to call work. Fresh-picked vegetables from your own garden are satisfying to the spirit and exciting to the senses. However, harvesting does have its moments of chore-like effort and that should be taken into account when you're planning your garden.

If you have a large crop of greens, for example, you may want to regularly harvest their leaves, which can require long periods of bending over the plants. Beans are another example of a crop whose harvesting can require time and labor. To keep beans producing, mature beans must be constantly picked, or the plant will stop producing. Overall, crops often ripen at the same time, keeping gardeners busy picking, preparing, and preserving (and eating!).

Chapter 3
Earth-Friendly Basics

Organic gardening is a return to gardening methods used before the 1950s, before the introduction of synthetic fertilizers and pesticides. It is a return to gardening in concert with nature, rather than fighting against it. Organic gardening combines knowledge of nature's cycles, patient observations, skilled guesses, and calm resolve; it is not a precise practice. When done properly, it can take far less energy and financial resources than non-organic methods. The gardening basics presented in this chapter will get you started and show you how uncomplicated and relaxing organic gardening can be. The basic rule of organic gardening is to tend first to your soil; all will follow easily after that.

Soil Cultivation

Cultivating your garden includes testing or analyzing the soil, amending it if needed, and turning your soil in the spring to loosen it and ready it for planting. When planting in a garden space for the first time, it is recommended that you have your soil tested.

Testing the Soil

Performing a soil test on samples of soil from your garden will give you information on its overall fertility, specifically the nutrient level, the soil structure (e.g., heavy clay, sandy, or a blend) and the pH level (a measure of how acidic or alkaline the soil is—most vegetables prefer a slightly acidic pH level). A soil test is the gold standard in soil analysis; it can be performed by your county's Extension Service or with a kit purchased at your local or online garden center.

With experience, however, you can perform a simple assessment of your soil using sight, touch, and smell—this may provide you with a "good enough" analysis. To assess your soil by its look and feel, get a handful of soil and make a fist. Good soil should be dark in color, crumble easily in your hand, retain a small amount of moisture, and have a rich, earthy, but not overpowering smell. Heavy clay will form a wet, sticky ball and very sandy soil will not hold together.

Amending the Soil

Whether from a soil test or direct observation, once you know the makeup of your soil you can amend it as needed, boosting your chances of a successful garden season. Soil amendments typically added in early spring include organic matter (compost, coffee grounds, leaf mulch, etc.), organic fertilizers (composted animal manures, worm castings, bone meal, greensand) and materials that will affect the pH balance (peat moss or lime). Most of these items can be purchased at garden centers or through catalogs, but items such as leaf mulch and coffee grounds may be available in bulk for free and can be saved up throughout the year and added all at once to the garden in the fall or early spring. Compost materials may be added to the soil liberally—try to add a minimum of 1 inch to the top of the bed and use a shovel or a digging fork to work into the soil. Organic fertilizers and materials that alter the soil pH are used in limited quantities; these products can burn your plants if used in high concentrations in the soil. Follow the directions on the packaging.

Turning the Soil

Turning the soil is a labor of love for a gardener, but it can be time consuming and hard on the back if you're not used to it. For a traditional garden dug directly into the soil, or a low raised bed, it is important for the health of your back to use the proper tools. Choose a long handled shovel with a round, pointed blade to turn the soil. If you need to remove grass to establish your garden, it is helpful to have a spading shovel, using its square flat edged blade to cut through the grass.

When working in established low raised beds or traditional garden beds, it is also helpful to have a garden fork with its sturdy, pointed prongs. This tool easily breaks up soil clumps and easily penetrates hard-packed soils. As the season progresses, a garden fork is also invaluable in reducing the effort needed to remove the deep-rooted weeds that invariably find their way into the garden.

There are two primary approaches to turning soil in a garden: random and methodical. Regardless of which method you choose, make sure to remove weeds, roots, and rocks as you go along, as well as chopping up any large soil clumps you dig up. (Hint: it is a easiest to turn hard-packed clay soils a few days after a thorough soaking from a rain storm, when the soil is still somewhat moist but not soggy.)

The random approach is quite simple: just turn over the soil one shovel at a time in any order you wish, flipping it and putting it back where it came from until the entire plot has been turned. This loosens and aerates the soil and exposes rocks for easy removal.

Methodically turning over the soil is a wonderfully thorough way of making sure every inch of the soil is turned, every rock unearthed, and every clump of soil broken up. This method is most useful on land that hasn't been cultivated in a while. Begin by dividing the garden bed in rows about the width of your shovel. Then, remove the soil from the first row and place it outside of the garden, ideally in a wheelbarrow or onto a tarp. Dig the soil from the second row and, flipping it, fill the space created by emptying the first row. Remove the soil from the third row, putting it into the empty space of the second row. Continue moving soil from one row into the preceding empty row until you've moved the last row into the next to last row. Finally, fill the very last row with the soil you removed from the first row, the soil you placed in a wheelbarrow or on a tarp.

Seeds and Starts

A garden can be planted from either seeds or *starts* (also called *transplants*). Seeds can be planted directly in the garden when the weather is appropriate, or they can be sown indoors in late winter to get a head start for the shorter growing season of the lower Great Lakes region. Starts are plants that have been started from seeds and typically grown in a greenhouse, a garden center, or at home on a sunny window sill or under a grow light. Starts are planted directly into the garden.

Starting Seeds Indoors

Germinating seeds indoors is an activity that all gardeners try at least once. Starting your own seeds can save you money, but it can also be time consuming and, depending on how you go about it, the initial cost of getting set up can be more than you'd pay for starts. However, if you already have a light source—a sunny south facing window sill or grow lights—and you're not too fussy about having the best supplies for the job, then growing your own starts from seed can be cost effective.

The trick to starting seeds indoors inexpensively is to use common household items for your seed pots, and to forgo warming trays and other helpful but expensive supplies. Ideally your seed pots will be biodegradable, allowing you to plant the entire container, plant and all, directly into the soil. This will not only save time when you move the starts into the garden, but also help you avoid root shock (disturbing the tiny, hair-like, root structures), enhancing the plant's ability to get down to the business of growing.

One suggestion for seed pots is small, unwaxed paper cups, such as Dixie bathroom cups. Another possibility is to use the cardboard tubes in toilet paper and paper towel rolls (cut the paper towel tube in half, giving you two tubes of equal length). Stand these paper tubes upright in a container with a waterproof bottom (a cardboard box lined with a plastic tray works well), fill the tubes with soil, and plant your seeds directly in them.

It is highly recommended that you use potting mix when starting seeds indoors. Potting mix contains no soil and provides an ideal medium for seed germination. It is sterile, guaranteeing your seeds will not be affected by soil-borne viruses and diseases. Make sure to water your seeds and emerging seedlings consistently, but moderately; they will die off easily if they are either waterlogged or dehydrated.

Direct Sowing in the Garden

Not all seeds can be successfully planted ahead of time indoors. Peas, for example, need cold to initiate their growth and do best when directly sown into the cold spring soil. Corn, cucumbers, and the entire squash family are vegetables that prefer to be started from seeds outdoors, due to the difficulty in transplanting them without damaging their roots. Root vegetables, such as carrots and radishes, are also typically directly sown into the garden, again to prevent damaging their roots. However, starting vegetables with sensitive roots in long paper tubing (see above) and planting the entire tube directly in the garden gets around the problem of root damage during transplanting.

Seed Hills

The seeds of some vegetables, notably cucumbers and squash, are often planted in groups of two or three, also known as *hills*. Because these plants need more than average organic matter in the soil, the ground is prepared in a unique way. First, a hole approximately

2 feet wide and 1 foot deep is dug. The soil removed from this hole is amended with an equal amount of compost and returned to the hole. The seeds are then planted several inches apart (see seed packets for directions) in the prepared soil.

Choosing Starts

When purchasing young plants, it takes a bit of experience to quickly identify which plants are healthy and which are sickly or too small to easily take hold in your garden. Plant size, leaf quality, quantity, color, and cleanliness are all important. Ideally, the size of the plant should be the same as the height of its pot. In evaluating the size of the start, look for plants that are at least 4 inches in height, but avoid ones that are so tall that they have become "leggy."

A leggy plant is usually tall and skinny, with far too few leaves for its height, appearing awkwardly tall and unbalanced. A plant that is leggy is often root bound, an indication it has been growing in the pot far too long, outgrowing the size of its pot. If you suspect a start is root bound, examine the bottom of the pot to see if roots are poking out of the drainage hole, or notice if the roots are massing above the soil, near the stem of the plant.

The quality of the start's leaves is also important; the leaves should be green, not yellow, brown, or black. That said, a few yellow leaves on the bottom of the plant is not highly unusual, and should not be of concern if the plant appears healthy otherwise. Finally, check the plant thoroughly for cleanliness: examine the underside of the leaves to make sure there isn't an infestation of insects, and check for mold or other unusual fungal problems on the leaves as well. And, if you just can't decide whether a start is healthy or not and you're in the middle of the store trying to decide, try asking another customer for an opinion—you might be surprised how willing your fellow gardeners are to help.

Hardening Off

When planting from starts, either homegrown or purchased, it is important that they *harden off* before planting in the garden. To do this, leave the plants outside for a few days in a covered location, away from direct sun exposure. Then, every few days for a week expose the plants to more sunshine. Start with a few hours of exposure, moving the plants back under shelter for the remainder of the day, and increase the exposure over several days or a week. Keep the plants well watered during this time. If temperatures drop to 45°F (7°C) or below, bring the plants back inside. When the outside temperatures have warmed up enough to be suitable for your plant (see seed packet for this information), transplant the starts into the garden.

Planting Starts

Planting starts in the garden is easy: simply dig a hole deep enough to plant the start at the same depth it was growing in the pot. Without pulling on the stem of the plant, dislodge the root mass from the pot.

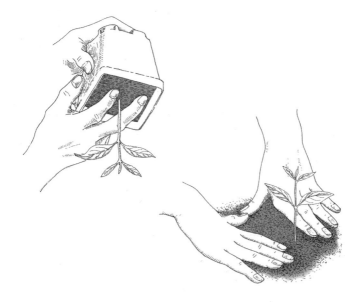

If the plant is root bound, gently tease apart the out roots so new soil and water can easily penetrate. Place the plant in the hole, and fill in around the plant with soil, tamping the soil lightly. Water thoroughly. If you can, it's best to transplant starts on cloudy days or early in the evening, when the sun is the least intense.

Multiple Crops: Cool vs. Warm Season Crops

Vegetables are classified as warm season plants, cool season plants, or both. A cool season plant is one that either needs cold temperatures to germinate and grow or one that does not thrive in the intense heat of the summers in the lower Great Lakes region. These vegetables can be planted in the early spring and again in the late summer. A warm season plant likes heat and needs a long growing season (from seed to fruit production); it stops production when cool weather arrives. Warm season vegetables are often started by seed indoors and planted outside in early summer. A vegetable that is classified as both a warm and a cool season crop can be grown in the lower Great Lakes region from early spring through late fall. These vegetables are often planted twice, once in early spring and again in early summer, producing two crops in the same season.

Cool Season	Warm Season	Both Warm and Cool
beets	beans	collards
brussels sprouts	cucumbers	Swiss chard
carrots	edamame	
kale	leeks	
leaf lettuce	peppers	
peas	summer squash	
radishes	winter squash	
spinach	tomatillos	
	tomatoes	

Succession Planting

Knowing what season your vegetable plant prefers is fundamental to growing it successfully. To double your garden's productivity, plant cool season spring crops, followed by a planting of warm season crops, followed by another planting of cool season crops. This method of gardening, called *succession planting*, is often used in raised-bed and container gardening, but less often in traditional garden beds. There is, however, no reason not to take advantage of this planting method in traditional garden beds, especially if your space is limited.

Companion Planting

Over time, gardeners have learned that some plants protect or enhance other plants if they are planted together; some deter insects while others improve the nutritional level of the soil. Companion planting is the pairing of plants in the garden that offer survival benefits to one or both of the plants. One well-known companion pairing is chives and roses. Chives (and, in fact, the entire onion family) repel aphids. Roses are often infested with aphids and growing chives among roses reduces the aphid population, reducing the need for chemical pest control. Some of the more common companion plantings found in the vegetable garden include:

- Basil planted among tomatoes to repel flies and improve flavor.
- Chives planted among tomatoes and carrots to help reduce aphids.
- Garlic planted among radishes to reduce aphids.
- French marigolds planted throughout the garden to kill Mexican bean beetles, soil-borne nematodes (parasitic worms that naturally inhabit the soil, harming the roots when their population is out of balance), and other insects.
- Nasturtiums planted throughout the garden to attract beneficial insects. Often planted with squash and pumpkins, nasturtiums deter squash bugs and striped pumpkin beetle.
- Parsley to attract bees to aid the pollination of flowering vegetables.
- Pepper plants planted throughout the garden to help deter viruses.
- Radishes planted among cucumbers to deter the cucumber beetle.
- Tomatoes planted among asparagus to repel the asparagus beetle.

Trellising and Staking

Trellises are essential for vegetables like peas and pole beans because these plants naturally grow vertically but need an upright support to do so. However, you can also train other vegetables, like cucumbers and some squash, to grow upward on a trellis, saving space in the garden. In both cases, upright supports can be essential tools for a successful harvest.

Trellises can also be used to add visual appeal to the garden. For example, adding a tepee-shaped trellis to a winding garden path introduces an interesting destination in a garden walk. Made from any number of materials, such as bamboo, cedar stakes, sticks, or metal stakes, and in any design, trellises can be quite artful.

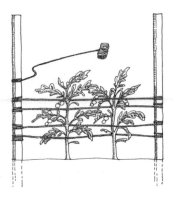

Staking is another way of supporting plants that like to grow vertically; it's particularly useful for plants with a heavy central stalk or weighty fruit. Brussels sprouts and tomatoes are two large plants that benefit from strong staking. There are various ways to stake, but the simplest is to place a single stake alongside the central stalk of the plant at the time of planting and tie the plant loosely to the stake with a soft twine or rag strip. Try to pound your stake 8–10 inches into the ground for the best support.

Staking a tomato patch is almost an art, with as many different methods as there are varieties of tomatoes. One space-saving method is called *stake and weave*. Begin a row by planting one or two tomato plants between 6-foot stakes. Leave 2 feet between plants and set stakes a foot from plants and a foot deep; always end a row with a stake. As the tomatoes grow, weave twine in and out of the plants and stakes, adding rows of twine every 6 inches as the plants grow taller.

Watering

Perhaps the most critical gardening component, watering is also the hardest to consistently get right. Mother Nature is constantly throwing too much or too little rain our way, making it difficult to know just how much water is needed at any given time.

Using a rain gauge is a great solution, but to be an effective tool the gauge must be emptied on a regular basis and the rainfall amount recorded for reference. An easier approach is to observe the plants and soil for signs of wilting and dryness, knowing that plants grown in this region need to receive about an inch of water once a week, either through watering or rainfall.

Water Deeply

When you water your garden, make sure to water it deeply; it is far better to water less frequently, but more thoroughly, than to water often, but shallowly. Watering for short periods, even frequently, will not allow water to reach far enough below the surface, causing the deeper roots to turn upward in an attempt to reach the water near the surface. Plants that have been watered shallowly will eventually die from water stress (always a surprise, as we thought they'd been well watered), or they will unexpectedly fall over because their roots are too shallow.

Fertilizing Plants

If you begin each season by amending your soil in early spring with organic materials high in nutrients such as compost, and organic fertilizers such as composted animal manure, bone meal, greensand and worm castings, you are unlikely to have to supplement with additional nutrients during the growing season. (However, fertility can become depleted more quickly in container gardens because plants have limited soil from which to find their nutrients.)

Whether in garden beds or containers, if individual plants appear to be stressed—losing leaves, showing discoloration in the leaves, having stunted growth, or otherwise not thriving—it may help to feed them fish emulsion or liquid seaweed. (Typically, bone meal and greensand are not added once the garden is planted.)

Fish Emulsion and Liquid Seaweed

Fish emulsion is high in nitrogen, encouraging leaf production. Liquid seaweed is high in both nitrogen and potassium, encouraging leaf and root production. Both of these fertilizers are concentrated liquids which must be diluted and used according to directions so they don't burn your plants.

Weeding

Weeding is a job few gardeners can escape. However, it can be reduced by taking a few precautions and knowing some facts about how weeds grow. Weeds, like most garden plants, are either annuals or perennials. It is not important to recognize each weed by name, but it is important to recognize an annual from a perennial.

Annuals complete their reproductive cycle in a single growing season. They grow, reproduce by flowering and then dropping their seeds or dispersing them into the air, and then quickly die. Annuals can be easily recognized by the abundance of flowers they produce. On the other hand, perennials spread and thrive by root growth, either producing a deep taproot or sending out new roots just under the surface to form new plants. Perennial weeds tend to be all leaf and stalk with few, if any, flowers.

Preventing Annual Weeds

Eliminating annual weeds from the garden requires that they are either prevented from going to seed or their seeds are prevented from germinating. You can do this by smothering them (preventing sunlight from reaching the soil by covering the garden space with black plastic or mulch), or by chemically damaging the seed using a natural pre-emergent (an herbicide which prevents the seed from germinating). Corn gluten is a derivative of corn that has pre-emergent properties when applied to soil in concentration. It is one of the few organic pre-emergents available on the market and is sold at garden centers.

One mistake often made in the fight against annual weeds is hoeing the garden regularly. Hoeing provides the immediate satisfaction of destroying any existing annual weeds but it has the disadvantage of bringing up new seeds, exposing them to the sun and starting a new round of seed germination. If you need to hoe your garden, cover the freshly disturbed soil with a heavy mulch or other sunlight barrier to discourage the newly unearthed seeds from sprouting.

Eliminating Perennial Weeds

Perennial weeds are more difficult to eradicate from the garden, but it can be done. Because this category of weed relies on its root structure for survival, the strategy is to exhaust the plant's energy stores, which are contained in the roots. Every time a portion of a perennial weed plant is pulled up or chopped off at the soil's surface, it causes the plant to send up new shoots, expending energy. Perennials replenish their energy through photosynthesis (the process a plant uses to form carbohydrates, requiring carbon dioxide, water and sunlight), which can only occur if the plant has leaves above the ground soaking up sunlight. To prevent this, cut off the leaves as soon as they poke above the ground. Eventually the plant will exhaust its energy stores and die back. Taproots on perennial weed plants have a significant energy store and it is likely to take a full season, cutting back these plants every three or four days, to eradicate these weeds. It's a daunting task for even the most dedicated gardener. The good news is that one season of effort will pay off in having far fewer perennial weeds to fight the next year.

Pests: Bugs, Blight, and the Four-Legged Pest

A basic tenet of keeping pests from becoming a problem in an organic garden is to keep the garden clean: remove dead plants, pick up leaves or other plant material that have molds, mildew or other fungi (spore producing parasites) on them, and discard plants that have been hard hit by insects. The idea is similar to a healthy immune system in an animal: viruses and bugs have a harder time attacking a healthy organism. For example, many plants have a thick waxy coating on their leaves that serves as a physical barrier to chewing insects. When the plant is stressed, that wax thins and chewing insects can gnaw right through. Making matters worse, these pests send out signals alerting others that they've found a source of food, attracting ever more insects to the plant. So, the best defense is to start with healthy soil and healthy plants, and to keep them that way by removing diseased or dying plants as soon as possible.

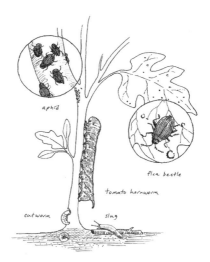

aphid

flea beetle

tomato hornworm

cutworm   slug

Insects and Organic Controls

The more common insects that cause gardeners grief are aphids, flea beetles, cutworms, slugs, and tomato hornworms. Two gentle organic methods of insect control are insecticidal soap (a weak soap solution that affects soft-bodied insects) and pepper spray (a mix of hot peppers and water). Insecticidal soap works well for aphids; pepper spray is used as a general repellent for chewing insects. Cutworms, slugs, and tomato hornworms are best just picked off the plant by hand, as they appear.

Recipes for Insect Control

Insecticidal Soap

1–2 TB liquid soap*

1 gallon water

Put mixture in a spray bottle and apply to affected areas every 7-10 days.

*It is important that you use pure soap, not liquid dish detergent. Ivory and Dr. Bronner's are examples of pure soaps.

Pepper Spray*

2 whole hot peppers

1 gallon plus 1 cup water

Purée hot peppers in a blender with 1 cup of water. Strain. Add this mixture to a gallon of water. Spray on plants as needed, reapplying after each watering or heavy rain.

*Wear rubber gloves and protect your eyes when making and working with this mixture.

If, despite your best efforts, your plants are being ravaged by bugs (eggplants are commonly attacked by flea beetles), you can resort to harsher organic chemical controls, like rotenone and pyrethrum (found at most garden centers). Make sure to read the label carefully, though, as these are strong chemicals.

Diseases

Some frequently seen diseases in the organic vegetable garden are powdery mildew, downy mildew, and verticillium wilt. Keeping the garden clean of leaves and plant matter that have been affected by these diseases is the best way to keep them from spreading. Do not add any part of a diseased plant to a home compost pile—discard the plant matter instead.

Animal Damage

And, finally, how can we prevent damage from four-legged pests? This is a topic gardeners spend long hours debating. Woodchucks, rabbits, deer, and our beloved dogs are the most damaging, but even squirrels can wreak havoc with their incessant digging in soft, newly planted soil and their desire to nibble on our vegetables just as they turn ripe. There are no perfect solutions. High raised beds, container gardens, wire mesh, and fencing are deterrents, but they can be costly both in time and money. To reduce rabbit and dog damage, try planting in raised beds or containers that are at least 18 inches high. Dogs, if they are not destructive to your garden, are wonderful at deterring rabbits.

For deer, one clever anti-deer fencing method I've come across is to build a double row of 4-foot high fencing, spaced 3–4 feet apart. The logic is that deer will not jump over the outer fence if it means their bellies will land on the second row of fencing. While I've never tried this solution, I have had good luck with a modification: use a single low fence and place raised beds 3 feet inside the fence. It's not perfect—gates tend to be left open and occasionally young deer try jumping the fence once before they learn—but it beats having an open garden where deer roam or incurring the expense of installing an 8-foot, unsightly fence.

For woodchucks and squirrels, there is very little other than trapping and relocating that seems to significantly reduce damage from these very resourceful creatures.

Harvesting

One of the most delightful reasons to grow your own vegetables is to experience the unique taste of freshly picked food. As an added benefit, vegetables are at their nutritional peak the moment they are picked. To get the most from your efforts, harvest vegetables as near to cooking as possible. If you need to store them before eating, keep them refrigerated.

Harvesting methods vary considerably, from digging or pulling up root vegetables, to shaking off dried seed heads from herbs, to twisting ripe fruit off the vine, to cutting fresh greens with a knife. Leaf lettuces cut to within an inch of the ground will bounce back with a full set of new leaves—this is called *cut and come again* harvesting.

Putting the Garden to Bed

Somewhere around mid- to late October, gardens in our region come to a seemingly abrupt end as the colder temperatures settle in: the plants stop producing new flowers, the fruit that remains is no longer growing larger, and the leaves hit by a hard frost are wilted. This is a sad time for most gardeners; it is a time to walk through the garden one last time harvesting what little produce is left, and it is a time to start the final chore of the season—putting the garden to bed. Putting the garden to bed is not difficult, but it does take a bit of physical effort. Although it has the feel of being a de-cluttering and cleaning exercise, its purpose is to prepare the garden for the following spring. For those who do not naturally seek order in their gardens, it might feel tempting to shun this last task. I urge you to ignore this tendency and recall the basic rule of organic gardening: tend first to your soil, and all will follow easily after that.

Clearing the Garden

When putting your garden to bed for the season, whether you have a traditional garden or garden in raised beds or containers, the first task is to remove the plant material. (Leave plants that come up in the spring like kale and garlic.) Remove the entire plant, roots and all, picking up any fallen leaves or fruit. This will reduce the chances of starting next spring with the same viruses and diseases you may have encountered this year.

Mulching the Soil

If you have a traditional or raised garden bed, once the garden is cleared of debris, turn or dig mulch into the soil to let it decompose over the winter (tree leaves make an excellent fall mulch). This effort will serve to improve the structure of your soil, again increasing your chances of success in the garden next season. Many gardeners lay a thick layer of straw over their garden as the final task of the season, almost literally putting a blanket over the bed for the winter. Covering the soil like this is not critical; however, it does offer the benefit of warming the soil a few weeks earlier in the spring than would occur otherwise, giving you a jump start on planting cool-weather crops such as peas, beets and kale.

Storing Containers

If you have a container garden and you started with the proper soil, you do not need to add mulch or amend the soil in the fall. If you used clay containers, be aware that they are not meant to withstand winter temperatures in this region. Remove the plant material and empty the pots of soil or move the whole pot, soil and all, into a protected space like a garage for the winter. Unless your container plant(s) had disease problems, store the soil for use again next spring.

Composting

Plant material that you remove from your garden at the end of the season (leaves, stems, roots, etc.) can be used to start or add to a compost pile, if you have room for it and the desire to maintain it next season. Composting is a detailed enough topic that it has generated a number of books and more than a few certification programs devoted to the practice. If you want to explore composting in a scientific or more methodical way, I encourage you to seek out additional information.

For now, though, if you'd like to get started composting in a simple and straightforward way, the most important thing to know is to alternate layers of organic materials in this ratio: 1 part nitrogen-rich materials (yard clippings, vegetable kitchen scraps, coffee grounds, manure) with 2 parts carbon-rich materials (straw, dried leaves, wood chips). Include a variety of particle sizes to ensure good air circulation.

Try piling dried leaves and twigs, spent plant matter, vegetable kitchen scraps, coffee grounds, and grass clippings in a somewhat shady area and water it once a week during the warm months so that it has the moisture of a wrung-out sponge. Turn it over a few times during the course of the summer to add oxygen, and then sit back and let nature do the rest. This method may take a few seasons for the denser matter in the pile to fully compost, so it's not the fastest composting method, but it is certainly the easiest.

You'll know that your compost is ready when the color is dark, the texture is fine and crumbly, and you can no longer distinguish the shape of the original materials you used.

Chapter 4
Recommended Vegetable Crops

Learning to garden is as much about learning what to plant as it is about how to grow it. This chapter presents a selection of the most common vegetables found in gardens throughout the lower Great Lakes region, chosen for their ease of care in the hands of a new gardener. A note of caution: throughout this book we use the word "vegetable" quite loosely. In everyday speaking, most of us casually refer to some fruits as vegetables and some vegetables as fruit. Botanically speaking, tomatoes, corn, and peas are fruit while rhubarb, used in pie filling, is a vegetable. The term "vegetable," as used in this book, refers to our common term for these plants, not their botanical classification.

The charts that begin on page 44 will give you an overview of how popular vegetable plants grow and what they need for successful production. This information will help in planning what to grow, where to grow it, and what to expect at harvest time. While this chapter includes enough information to start a garden, the information is limited by the introductory nature of this book. Carefully read the planting instructions provided on each of your seed packets or do some research on your starts.

The family names of each plant have been included because members of the same plant family tend to be affected by the same virus, fungal, and insect problems. This knowledge is useful even when you are planning your garden. For example, all members of the *Solanaceae* family (commonly called the "nightshade" family) are susceptible to the toxins in black walnut trees (juglans). This is a big family, including tomatoes, peppers, eggplants, and potatoes, and they must all be planted outside of the root and canopy spread of black walnut trees.

Seasoned gardeners often rotate where they plant their vegetables every year based on family classification rather than specific species within a family. This is because plants are also known as light, moderate, and heavy feeders, and related plants generally have similar nutrient needs. In addition, while some plants, such as beans and peas, tend to increase soil nutrients, others, such as peppers and tomatoes, tend to deplete them. As a new gardener, you should familiarize yourself with the general families of vegetables even though this information is not needed to get started.

Journal space is provided for each vegetable listed in this chapter. Keeping notes on what you planted and on how well individual varieties performed can provide invaluable information for future gardening seasons, reminding you what worked well and what didn't, how you tackled insect or pest damage, and what foods you enjoyed growing and what you would rather purchase from the grocery store. You might also want to make a note of which plants provided you with extra vegetables for family, friends, or food banks.

Making a simple drawing of what was planted where is also a good idea. When you come back to your garden the following spring, this information can be used to rotate your crops to different areas of the space.

A journal can also be a place to record the small but easily forgotten joys of gardening: what it felt like putting your hands in the warmed summer soil, seeing the first butterfly of the season, the aroma of crushed mint leaves, or how the squirrels chattered away in the background as you worked. A journal is particularly helpful in your first few years as a gardener, as you learn how to garden and how to feel comfortable and joyous in the garden spaces you're creating.

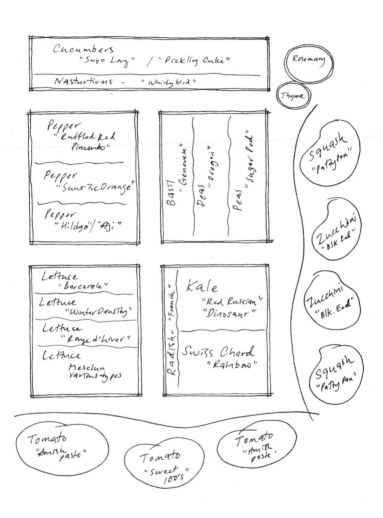

Cucumbers
"Suyo Long" / "Pickling Cuke"

Nasturtiums - "Whirlybird"

Rosemary

Thyme

Pepper
"Ruffled Red Pimento"

Pepper
"SunBeOrange"

Pepper
"Hidalgo"/ "Aji"

Basil "Genovese"

Peas "Oregon"

Peas "Sugar Pod"

Squash "Patty Pan"

Zucchini "Blk End"

Zucchini "Blk End"

Squash "Patty Pan"

Lettuce
"Barcarole"

Lettuce
"Winter Density"

Lettuce
"Rouge d'hiver"

Lettuce
Mesclun
Various types

Radish "French"

Kale
"Red Russian"
"Dinosaur"

Swiss Chard
"Rainbow"

Tomato
"Amish paste"

Tomato
"Sweet 100's"

Tomato
"Amish paste"

Sample Garden Map

Beans, Snap
Leguminosae family

Cool or warm season:	warm
Begin with:	seeds; sow directly in the garden
Grows as:	an annual: bush and pole varieties available
Plant size:	see seed packet; from dwarf to 8'
Plant outside:	early to late May
Sun and location:	full sun
Soil type preferred:	well drained
Planting depth:	1" in clay soils, 1.5" in sandy soils
Spacing at planting:	2", thin to 4" apart; 18"–24" between rows
Container plant:	yes, with 6" minimum soil depth
Days to harvest:	50–70
Yield per 10' row:	approximately 5 lbs.
Harvest season:	mid-July through mid-September

There are many varieties of beans, and they grow as either bush or pole (runner) beans. Snap, or green beans, are eaten fresh while others are dried for long-term storage.

Suggested varieties:
Bush: Blue Lake, Royal Purple, Rocdor (yellow wax round pod).
Pole: Kentucky Wonder, Romano (Italian), Purple Podded Pole.

Planting hints:
Beans don't like soggy soils—plant where the soil dries out between waterings. They produce nitrogen and do not require nitrogen-rich amendments, like composted manure, or fertilizers, like fish emulsion.

Beans are sensitive to salt in the soil—avoid planting locations close to streets, which may have been salted during winter months.

Growing hints:

Beans grow best when temperatures are between 70°F and 80°F (21°–27°C).

Except for bush varieties, beans need to be trellised to keep their leaves dry and healthy, as well as for ease of harvesting. See page 30 for more information.

Harvesting hints:

Snap beans are most tender before the seeds in their pods start to bulge. They can become tough if left on the vine too long. Beans tend to be prolific producers and individual beans ripen quickly. Pick beans frequently, at least every 3 days, to encourage continued production.

Journal

Variety planted:

Date planted (seeds or starts):

Location:

Date of first harvest:

Notes:

Beets
Chenopodiaceae family

Cool or warm season:	cool
Begin with:	seeds; sow directly in the ground
Grows as:	an annual: individual plants, one beet per plant
Plant size:	approximately 18" tall
Plant outside:	spring through mid summer
Sun and location:	sun to semi-shade
Soil type preferred:	loose to semi-clay, well-drained
Planting depth:	1/2" deep
Spacing at planting:	2", thin to 4" apart; 18"–24" between rows
Container plant:	yes, with 6" minimum soil depth
Days to harvest:	60–80
Yield per 10' row:	approximately 10 lbs.
Harvest season:	midsummer through late fall

This plant is one of my favorites for several reasons: it produces two crops in one (greens and beets), is an ideal container plant, grows in shadier spots where few other vegetables will grow, and is, overall, one of the most carefree vegetables to grow in the garden.

Suggested varieties:
Detroit Red (red), Golden (yellow), Chioggia (red and white interior).

Planting hints:
The beet seeds found in seed packets are actually fruit pods containing many tiny beet seeds. Don't overdo planting beets, as each pod is likely to germinate significantly more than you recall planting.

Growing hints:

Because beet seed pods contain so many seeds, you will need to thin your beet seedlings to ensure that individual plants have room to grow. Don't be afraid to take out the extra seedlings; it's better to have a few good-sized beets than a large number of small, misshapen ones. You can thin in stages, keeping in mind that beets need about 4 inches between plants.

Harvesting hints:

The leaves of the beet are called "beet greens," and can be harvested at any time. Cut no more than one third of the greens at any one time and don't cut again until new leaves have sprouted.

Beet roots can also be harvested at any time, but I recommend letting them reach at least 1 inch in diameter (the top of the beet will be poking above the soil's surface). Beets left in the ground after they fully mature tend to become tough, so try not to let the root become too large.

Journal

Variety planted:

Date planted (seeds or starts):

Location:

Date of first harvest:

Notes:

Brussels Sprouts
Cruciferae family

Cool or warm season:	cool
Begin with:	seeds or starts
Grows as:	an annual, with sprouts growing on the stalk
Plant size:	approximately 3' tall
Plant outside:	seeds, late May–early June; starts, mid-July
Sun and location:	full sun
Soil type preferred:	well-drained with organic material
Planting depth:	1/2" for seeds, see hints below for starts
Spacing at planting:	seeds: 6", thin to 2' apart; 30" between rows
Container plant:	no
Days to maturity:	seeds, approximately 100; starts, 55–75
Yield per 10' row:	approximately 2.5 lbs.
Harvest season:	late fall, early winter

Brussels sprouts are best grown as a fall crop. They are one of the families (*brassica* and *crucifeae*) known as *cole crops*. Like others in this group, they taste better after a few light frosts. Choose a short season variety that will mature before winter weather sets in.

Suggested varieties:
Bubbles, Long Island Improved.

Planting hints:
If using starts, set the plants deeper than they were planted in their pots, placing the lowest leaves just above the soil line.

Growing hints:

If starting with seeds outdoors, thin plants when they are about 6 inches tall, spacing them so they are approximately 2 feet apart. Brussels sprouts have shallow roots and they need to be weeded carefully. They are also susceptible to being blown over by strong winds; if you have a windy site, place a stake near the plant and tie it loosely to the stalk.

Harvesting hints:

Brussels sprouts become sweeter after a few light frosts, so pick these tender mini-cabbages late in the season. You can pick the individual sprouts, beginning with the sprouts at the bottom of the stalk, or you can harvest them all at once by cutting or pulling up the entire stalk. The mature sprouts look like tiny cabbages—firm and a little shiny. Usually the sprouts on the bottom of the stalk are smaller when mature, but don't wait for them to get bigger; if they start to open, you've waited too long.

Journal

Variety planted:

Date planted (seeds or starts):

Location:

Date of first harvest:

Notes:

Carrots
Umbelliferae family

Cool or warm season:	cool
Begin with:	seeds
Grows as:	an annual; individual plants; one carrot per plant
Plant size:	6" to 12" tall
Plant outside:	early spring, planting again every 2 weeks
Sun and location:	full sun
Soil type preferred:	loose soil
Planting depth:	broadcast seeds, cover with a 1/4" layer of soil
Spacing at planting:	thin seedlings to at least 2" between plants
Container plant:	yes, with 8" minimum soil depth
Days to harvest:	65–85
Yield per 10' row:	approximately 10 lbs.
Harvest season:	summer through fall

Homegrown carrots rarely reach the length of those seen in markets. Those are grown in extremely sandy soils, which allow long roots to develop. Shorter varieties work best for home gardeners.

Suggested varieties:
Thumbelina (a small round carrot—great in containers), Napoli.

Planting hints:
Carrot seeds are quite small, making them difficult to handle individually. It is easiest to broadcast seeds over loose soil and cover them with a 1/4-inch layer of soil. As with most cool-weather plants, you can plant a new row of carrots every 2 weeks throughout the summer.

Growing hints:

Carrot seeds can take up to 3 weeks to germinate. To ensure that the root will have enough room to develop, you will need to thin the seedlings as they grow. You can thin in stages, keeping in mind that carrots need about 2 inches between plants and 18–24 inches between rows. Don't be afraid to cut or pull up the extras; as with beets, it's better to have a few good sized carrots than a large number of small, misshapen, and unappetizing ones.

Harvesting hints:

Determining when carrots are ready to harvest is a bit of an art. Wait until you see the top of the carrot poking above the soil's surface by about a 1/2 inch, then pull up one or two carrots to see if the roots are large enough. Carrots can be eaten at any size, so it's a matter of personal preference when you harvest; however, they can become tough and cracked if left in the ground too long once fully mature.

Journal

Variety planted:

Date planted (seeds or starts):

Location:

Date of first harvest:

Notes:

Collard Greens & Kale

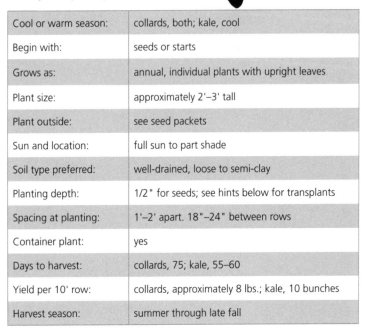

Cruciferae family

Cool or warm season:	collards, both; kale, cool
Begin with:	seeds or starts
Grows as:	annual, individual plants with upright leaves
Plant size:	approximately 2'–3' tall
Plant outside:	see seed packets
Sun and location:	full sun to part shade
Soil type preferred:	well-drained, loose to semi-clay
Planting depth:	1/2 " for seeds; see hints below for transplants
Spacing at planting:	1'–2' apart. 18"–24" between rows
Container plant:	yes
Days to harvest:	collards, 75; kale, 55–60
Yield per 10' row:	collards, approximately 8 lbs.; kale, 10 bunches
Harvest season:	summer through late fall

Unlike kale, collards can tolerate heat and can be planted throughout the summer. Kale is best grown as a fall crop. Like all cole crops, collards and kale become sweeter after a light frost.

Suggested varieties:
Collards: Champion.
Kale: Red Russian, Dinosaur/Lacinato, Winterbor, Dwarf Siberian.

Planting hints:
Collard greens and kale, like other dark greens, prefer a semi-shady area. Plant them in the shade of another garden vegetable, like toma-

toes, or where a nearby tree can provide shade during the heat of the summer.

Growing hints:
Collard greens and kale are well suited for container gardening, as long as they receive adequate watering throughout the season.

Rabbits like to nibble on all greens, including collard greens and kale. You may need to protect them with netting or fencing, or plant them in a raised bed or container at least 18 inches tall.

Harvesting hints:
Cut the leaves throughout the growing season as you wish, making sure not to take more than 1/3 of the plant at any one cutting.

Collard greens become sweeter after a heavy frost, so for a taste treat leave enough of your crop uncut until after the cold weather hits. Snow does not bother this plant, but it will die back once temperatures remain at or below freezing for the winter.

Journal

Variety planted:

Date planted (seeds or starts):

Location:

Date of first harvest:

Notes:

Cucumber
Cucurbitaceae family

Cool or warm season:	warm
Begin with:	seeds or starts in peat pots
Grows as:	an annual, a vine
Plant size:	approximately 6' spread
Plant outside:	2 weeks after the last frost
Sun and location:	full sun
Soil type preferred:	well-drained soil with organic material added
Planting depth:	seeds, 1"; transplants, root line
Spacing at planting:	1' apart
Container plant:	yes, with 10" minimum soil depth
Days to harvest:	50–70
Yield per 10' row:	approximately 6 lbs.
Harvest season:	late summer, early fall

Some cucumbers have male and female flowers on a single plant and others have male and female plants mixed together in seed packets. They all rely on pollination by bees. The male flowers drop off and the female flowers turn into the fruits.

Suggested varieties:
Burpless, Spartan Salad and Diva (slicing); Northern Pickling and Little Leaf (pickling); Lemon (both slicing and pickling).

Planting hints:
Cucumbers have sensitive roots and don't like transplanting. If starting plants indoors, use peat pots, which can be planted directly in the ground. Cucumber seeds are often planted in hills about 4 feet apart,

with 3–7 seeds placed in each hill. This method protects the seeds from rotting in the ground during the frequent spring rains.

If growing space is limited, consider trellising your cucumber plants (see page 30). This method can also help reduce viruses, as the wind dries the plant's leaves better when the vines are upright and off the ground.

Growing hints:
Try to water cucumbers close to their roots and avoid splashing the leaves with water. Damp conditions can invite *powdery mildew* (see page 35), which damages the plant's health.

Harvesting hints:
Check your plant every couple of days, picking cucumbers before they become too large or begin to turn yellow. Cucumbers must be picked before they are fully developed because even a single fruit reaching maturity can cause the plant to stop growing. To compound matters, once this plant starts to produce, the cucumbers come fast and furiously. If the plant produces more fruit than you can use at one time, consider donating them to your local food bank or to neighbors.

Journal

Variety planted:

Date planted (seeds or starts):

Location:

Date of first harvest:

Notes:

Edamame / Soybeans
Leguminosae family

Cool or warm season:	warm
Begin with:	seeds sown directly in the ground
Grows as:	an annual, bush
Plant size:	12"–30" tall
Plant outside:	on or after date of last frost
Sun and location:	full sun
Soil type preferred:	well-drained, high in organic matter
Planting depth:	1" in heavy soils, 1.5" in loose soils
Spacing at planting:	2' apart
Container plant:	yes, with 6" minimum soil
Days to harvest:	approximately 90
Yield per 10' row:	approximately 5 lbs.
Harvest season:	summer

Edamame is another name for soybeans, but it refers specifically to the beans and pods when they are still green and tender, rather than the dried beans that most of us identify with soybeans.

Suggested varieties:

Butterbeans, Beer Friend.

Planting hints:

All beans need to have certain bacteria present in the soil in order for the seed to germinate, but soybeans seem to be a bit more fussy on this point. Good compost provides a full spectrum of the various bacteria beans need to sprout, so if planting in soil amended with compost this requirement should not be a concern. If planting in soil with little organic matter (sand, clay, or potting mix), you might consider inoculating the beans before planting. Inoculates are a dried form of beneficial soil bacteria—they come either as a powder used to coat the seeds before planting, or as a granule that is added to the soil before planting. Inoculant can be purchased at most garden centers and online.

Growing hints:

Soybeans grow best when temperatures are between 70°–80°F (21°–27°C). Like most beans, they have no significant pests, making them an easy plant to tend in the garden.

Harvesting hints:

For edamame, pick the beans when they are still green and tender; they can be eaten fresh from the vine (shell first; the pods are not edible). For dried soybeans, let the beans fully dry on the vine.

Soybeans, like other bush beans, produce all at once. This trait allows you to pull or dig up entire plants and move them into the shade, where you can then pick the beans from the comfort of a chair.

Journal

Variety planted:

Date planted (seeds or starts):

Location:

Date of first harvest:

Notes:

Leeks
Liliaceae family

Cool or warm season:	warm
Begin with:	seeds or starts
Grows as:	a biennial grown as an annual; individual stalk
Plant size:	approximately 12" tall
Plant outside:	when night temps are at or above 60°F (15°C)
Sun and location:	full sun
Soil type preferred:	loose, with organic matter
Planting depth:	transplant to first set of leaves or in trenches
Spacing at planting:	6" apart
Container plant:	no
Days to maturity:	seeds: 90–120; starts: 70–100
Yield per 10' row:	approximately 5 lbs.
Harvest season:	mid to late fall

Leeks are related to onions, but have a sweeter flavor and are resistant to many of the pests and diseases that can make onions difficult to grow. They are attractive grown en masse.

Suggested varieties:
Giant Musselburgh, Bandit, Fall Leek, King Richard.

Planting Hints:
Leeks are easy to grow, but because they need a long growing season, gardeners have the best luck starting with starts. If you wish to

start them from seed, sow them indoors 2–3 months before the last expected frost.

Growing hints:
The white portion of the stalk has a more delicate flavor than the green leaves. To encourage more white stalk on the leek, many gardeners plant them in the bottom of a 6-inch trench and pile up soil at the base of the stalks as they grow. This blanches the leeks (keeps the stalks white and tender). Another way to blanch them is to bury the leek to the base of the first leaf joint when transplanting.

Harvesting hints:
You can harvest baby leeks any time you like by pulling them out of the soil. For mature leeks, dig them out when they are no more than 1 inch in diameter, usually near the end of the growing season. Leeks become sweeter after a light frost but a heavy frost will kill them, so harvest before the weather turns severe.

Journal

Variety planted:

Date planted (seeds or starts):

Location:

Date of first harvest:

Notes:

Lettuce, leaf
Compositae family

Cool or warm season:	cool
Begin with:	seeds or starts
Grows as:	an annual, individual plants
Plant size:	generally less than 18"
Plant outside:	once soil temperatures are above freezing
Sun and location:	sun in spring and fall; shade in summer
Soil type preferred:	well-drained, high in organic matter
Planting depth:	broadcast seeds and do not cover
Spacing at planting:	thin plants to 6" apart; 12"–18" between rows
Container plant:	yes, with 6" minimum soil
Days to harvest:	45-55
Yield per 10' row:	approximately 5 lbs.
Harvest season:	early summer, fall

Lettuce tastes best when grown in cool weather. Though there are a few varieties that can be grown in the summer, generally in hot weather lettuce wilts, becomes bitter, and quickly goes to seed.

Suggested varieties:
Black-seeded Simpson, Buttercrunch.

Planting hints:
Lettuce seeds are quite small and difficult to handle individually. It's easiest to broadcast the seeds over loose soil and simply push the

seeds gently into the soil. Lettuce seeds need light to germinate, so don't fully cover them with soil.

As with most cool-weather plants, you can plant lettuce again in the late summer for a fall crop.

Growing hints:
Because lettuce seeds are broadcast, you will need to thin the seedlings so that individual plants have room to grow. You can thin in stages if you wish, eating the lettuce plants you pull up in the later stages of the season.

Lettuce is frequently nibbled on by rabbits, so you might want to protect it with netting or fencing, or by planting it in a raised bed or container at least 18 inches high.

Harvesting hints:
To extend the harvesting period of individual lettuce plants, cut individual leaves from the plant as needed, rather than pulling up the entire plant. You can also cut the plant down to 1 inch high, and it will grow back to full size.

Journal

Variety planted:

Date planted (seeds or starts):

Location:

Date of first harvest:

Notes:

Peas
Leguminosae family

Cool or warm season:	cool
Begin with:	seeds
Grows as:	an annual, bush (dwarf), or vine
Plant size:	see seed packet, varies from 18"–24" to 6'
Plant outside:	approx. 4 weeks before last frost, again mid-July
Sun and location:	full sun, protect from high winds
Soil type preferred:	well-drained, loose
Planting depth:	1" in heavy soils, 2" in loose soils
Spacing at planting:	2"–3"; 12"–18" between rows
Container plant:	yes, with 8" minimum soil depth
Days to harvest:	55–70
Yield per 10' row:	approximately 2 1/2 lbs.
Harvest season:	early summer, late fall

Peas are one of the earliest vegetables to plant and harvest; they may even be ready to pick by Memorial Day and are often finished producing early in June! Some peas grow in thinner edible pods (sometimes called sugar or snow peas) and are eaten whole, while others need to be shelled first. Check your seed packet to learn what type you have.

Suggested varieties:
Edible pods: Snow Sweet, Oregon Sugar Pod II.
Shelling: Wando, Oregon Trail.

Planting hints:
Peas like cold weather and are typically planted well before spring has fully arrived. Plant peas directly in the garden in the early spring, once

the top 1–2 inches of the soil thaws. Soaking the seeds for 24 hours before planting can help germination.

The soil around peas can be interplanted with radishes, beets, carrots, and lettuce or other greens.

Growing hints:
Peas grow better in cooler temperatures; growth slows or stops altogether when temperatures reach 70°F (21°C).

Peas, and all legumes, produce their own nitrogen and are sensitive to added nitrogen in the soil. Go lightly if you use composted manures where you plant your peas and other legumes.

Harvesting hints:
Once peas start to produce, they need to be harvested continuously. Peas, like beans, will start to shut down production when they successfully produce mature seed (once the peas in the pods dry out). Check your plants at least once every three days.

Pick edible-podded varieties when the seeds inside are just starting to form. Harvest shelling peas when firm and well-filled, but before they reach full size and start to change color.

Journal

Variety planted:

Date planted (seeds or starts):

Where planted:

Location:

Notes:

Peppers
Solanaceae family

Cool or warm season:	warm
Begin with:	starts
Grows as:	an annual, bush
Plant size:	approximately 18" tall
Plant outside:	after all chances of frost are past (May 20–June 1)
Sun and location:	full sun
Soil type preferred:	well-drained, with organic matter
Planting depth:	plant to the same depth as it is in the pot
Spacing at planting:	2' apart
Container plant:	yes, with 8" minimum soil depth
Days to harvest:	from starts: 65–85
Yield per 10' row:	approximately 6 lbs.
Harvest season:	late summer or early fall

Peppers are tropical plants and need a long, warm summer to mature. If planting from transplants, expect a full 2 months or more before the plants start to produce fruit.

Suggested varieties:
Sweet (bell): North Star.
Hot: Anaheim, Jalapeño.

Planting hints:
There are two groups of peppers: hot and sweet. They can cross pollinate, so it's best not to plant them near each other.

Peppers are ideal plants for both container gardening and for planting here and there throughout your garden. They are members of the solanaceae family and are susceptible to the toxin in black walnut roots, so plant away from the roots and canopy of that tree.

Growing hints:
Peppers are relatively disease and insect free.

Harvesting hints:
Mature peppers easily snap off the plant when you gently twist them. Avoid pulling the fruit off—cut instead.

Sweet peppers typically start out green, changing colors to red, orange, or brown as it matures.The fruit can be eaten at any of these color stages, and it gets sweeter the longer it ripens. Hot peppers can go through even more color changes, depending on the variety, but they are typically harvested only after reaching full maturity.

Be careful when picking fresh hot peppers; the oils you pick up on your fingertips can be painful if you touch your eyes, lips, or other sensitive skin.

Journal

Variety planted:

Date planted (seeds or starts):

Location:

Date of first harvest:

Notes:

Radish
Cruciferae family

Cool or warm season:	cool
Begin with:	seeds
Grows as:	an annual; individual plants, one radish per plant
Plant size:	approximately 6" tall
Plant outside:	4 weeks before last frost, again every week
Sun and location:	full sun to light shade
Soil type preferred:	loose soil with organic matter
Planting depth:	1/2"
Spacing at planting:	1" apart, thin to 2-4"; 6"–12" between rows
Container plant:	yes, with 4" minimum soil depth
Days to harvest:	25–30
Yield per 10' row:	10 lbs.
Harvest season:	spring through fall

Small-rooted radishes are the most common in our region, but large-rooted varieties common in Europe and Asia can be grown here, too. All are wonderfully crisp and peppery. They are a great crop for experimenting with varieties.

Suggested varieties:
Champion, Cherry Belle.

Planting hints:
For a continuous supply of fresh radishes throughout the summer, plant new seeds every week from early spring until early summer, then start again in late summer for a fall harvest.

Growing hints:
Radishes need 2–4 inches between plants to form a root with good shape. Because radishes grow so quickly, it is important to thin them as soon as the seeds germinate.

Radish like soils high in organic matter, but they will form too many leaves and poor roots if the soil has too much nitrogen—use composted manures sparingly.

Harvesting hints:
Like carrots, determining when radishes are ready to harvest is a bit of an art. Wait until you see the top of the root poking above the soil surface, then pull up one or two to see if they are large enough. Radishes can be eaten at any size. Though it's a matter of personal preference when you harvest, radishes can become tough and cracked if left in the ground too long once fully mature.

Journal

Variety planted:

Date planted (seeds or starts):

Where planted:

Location:

Notes:

Spinach
Chenopodiaceae family

Cool or warm season:	cool
Begin with:	seeds or starts
Grows as:	an annual; individual plants with upright leaves
Plant size:	2'–3' tall
Plant outside:	early spring, again in late summer
Sun and location:	full sun to partial shade
Soil type preferred:	loose to semi-clay, well-drained
Planting depth:	1/4"–1/2" for seeds
Spacing at planting:	2" apart, thin to 6"; 12"–18" between rows
Container plant:	yes, with 8" minimum soil depth
Days to harvest:	from seeds: 40–50
Yield per 10' row:	approximately 5 lbs.
Harvest season:	midsummer and late fall

Spinach is a fast-growing crop related to beets and Swiss chard. It is native to Persia and was introduced to Europe around 1000 A.D.

Suggested varieties:
America, Viking.

Planting hints:
Spinach likes a lot of nitrogen in the soil. Because composted manure is a good source of nitrogen it is recommended that you add it to the soil before planting, but only in the top few inches, as spinach has relatively shallow roots.

Spinach cannot tolerate the heat of the summer sun and is typically grown in the cool spring for a midsummer harvest and planted again in the late summer for a second harvest in the fall.

Growing hints:
This plant is frequently nibbled on by rabbits, so you might need to protect it with netting or fencing, or plant it in a raised bed or container at least 18 inches tall.

Harvesting hints:
Cut the leaves throughout the growing season as you wish, making sure not to take more than 1/3 of the plant at any one cutting.

If you plant a late-summer crop of spinach for fall harvesting, it will become sweeter after a light frost.

Journal

Variety planted:

Date planted (seeds or starts):

Where planted:

Location:

Notes:

Squash, Summer
(Zucchini, Yellow, etc.)
Cucurbitaceae family

Cool or warm season:	warm
Begin with:	seeds or starts
Grows as:	a vine, which can be left on the ground or trellised
Plant size:	see seed packet, generally 6' long
Plant outside:	after all chances of frost are past
Sun and location:	full sun
Soil type preferred:	well-drained, with organic matter
Planting depth:	seeds, 1"–1 1/2"; starts, same depth as in pot
Spacing at planting:	varies by planting method
Container plant:	yes, with 10" minimum soil depth
Days to harvest:	45–60
Yield per 10' row:	approximately 10 lbs.
Harvest season:	late summer, early fall

Summer squash are notoriously prolific, and it's easy to plant more than you can eat. Plan on two plants for every four people you will be feeding.

Suggested varieties:
Zucchini Elite, Early Prolific, Straightneck, St. Pat Scallop.

Planting hints:
Summer squash seeds are often planted in hills (see page 25), with 3–4 seeds placed in each hill. This method helps protect the seeds from rotting in the ground during the frequent late spring rains. Space hills 3–4 feet apart.

Growing hints:

If growing space is limited, consider trellising your squash plants (see page 30) rather than using hills. This method can also help reduce viruses, as the wind dries the leaves better when the plants are upright. Try to water squash plants close to their roots and avoid splashing their leaves with water. Damp conditions can invite powdery mildew (see page 35), which damages the plant's health.

Harvesting hints:

Squash, like cucumbers, can be eaten at any size. However, they are at their best when still small, from 3 to 8 inches in length. Once the squash plant starts to produce, the fruit comes at an alarming rate. To keep the plant producing, continuously pick the ripe fruit. If one fruit becomes fully mature, the plant will slow or stop production. To avoid damaging the vine, it is best to cut off the summer squash rather than tearing or twisting it off.

Journal

Variety planted:

Date planted (seeds or starts):

Location:

Date of first harvest:

Notes:

Squash, Winter

(Acorn, Butternut, Hubbard, Spaghetti, etc.)
Cucurbitaceae family

Cool or warm season:	warm
Begin with:	starts
Grows as:	ground-hugging vine
Plant size:	10'–20' long
Plant outside:	after all chances of frost are past
Sun and location:	full sun to light shade
Soil type preferred:	well drained, with organic matter
Planting depth:	seeds, 1/2"; transplants, same depth as in pot
Spacing at planting:	6'–8' apart
Container plant:	yes, with 10" minimum soil
Days to harvest:	85–110
Yield per 10' row:	10–15 lbs.
Harvest season:	late fall, early winter

Winter squash can be difficult to grow because they require a very long growing season. Look for varieties that will produce in the shorter season that characterizes our region.

Suggested varieties:
Waltham Butternut, Buttercup, Table Queen.

Planting hints:
Winter squash seeds are often planted in hills (see page 25), with just 3–4 seeds placed in each hill. This elevated planting method protects the seeds from rotting in the ground during the frequent spring rains.

Planting in level ground is also fine if that suits your needs. For either method, plant the seed groupings 6–8 feet apart.

Growing hints:

By midsummer in our region, winter squash plants will have set all the flowers that can reasonably grow into mature fruit before the first frost. You can help ensure your winter squash fully ripens by pinching off any new flowers that appear on the vine after midsummer.

Harvesting hints:

Winter squash is ripe when the stem dries and the skin of the fruit hardens. A hard, killing frost will damage the fruit, so harvest before that point in the season. Use scissors or a knife to cut the fruit off the vine, leaving a good 1–2 inches of the stem on the ripe fruit. If the weather allows, leave the fruit outside in the sun for a week or two to cure. Cover at night if frost is predicted.

If the plant produces more fruit than you can use at one time, consider donating to your local food bank or giving to neighbors.

Journal

Variety planted:

Date planted (seeds or starts):

Location:

Date of first harvest:

Notes:

Swiss Chard
Chenopodiaceae family

Cool or warm season:	both
Begin with:	seeds or starts
Grows as:	individual plants with upright leaves
Plant size:	2'–3' tall
Plant outside:	early spring through late summer
Sun and location:	full sun to partial shade
Soil type preferred:	loose to semi-clay, well-drained
Planting depth:	seeds, 1/2"; starts, same depth as in pot
Spacing at planting:	plant seeds 2" apart, gradually thin to 10" apart
Container plant:	yes, with 8" minimum soil
Days to harvest:	from seed: 50–60
Yield per 10' row:	approximately 9 lbs.
Harvest season:	summer through late fall

Swiss chard is an ancestor of beets; it has the leafy greens of beets, but not the large edible root. It grows easily from seed and does well in both cool and warm seasons. In recent years, varieties with intensely colored stalks have been introduced. The visual interest created by these bright stalks makes Swiss chard a great candidate for edible landscaping.

Suggested varieties:
Rainbow, Rhubarb, Fordhook Giant.

Planting hints:

This green makes an ideal plant for partly shady areas. Try planting it in the shade of a deciduous tree.

Swiss chard is an excellent container plant.

Growing hints:

As with all greens, this plant is frequently nibbled on by rabbits, and containers (or raised beds) at least 18 inches tall can protect chard. Netting and fencing can also be used.

Make sure Swiss chard receives adequate water throughout the season.

Harvesting hints:

Cut the leaves throughout the growing season, making sure not to take more than 1/3 of the plant at any one time. Swish chard is tolerant of summer heat and is slow to go to seed, so it can be harvested all season.

Journal

Variety planted:

Date planted (seeds or starts):

Location:

Date of first harvest:

Notes:

Tomatillos
Solanaceae family - physalis ixocarpa

Cool or warm season:	warm
Begin with:	starts
Grows as:	an annual, a bush
Plant size:	approximately 2 1/2' tall
Plant outside:	after all chances of frost are past
Sun and location:	moderate to full sun
Soil type preferred:	well-drained, high in organic matter
Planting depth:	1/2" for seeds
Spacing at planting:	3' apart; 3' between rows
Container plant:	yes, with 12" minimum soil depth
Days to harvest:	60–75
Yield per 10' row:	8–10 lbs.
Harvest season:	late fall, early winter

Tomatillos are the main ingredient in Mexican green sauces. They are related to tomatoes, but their fruits are smaller and green or purple when ripe. Though this plant is native to Central and South America, it grows extremely well in the shorter season of our region.

Suggested varieties:
Green: Toma Verde.
Purple: Purple de Milpa.

Planting hints:
Tomatillos are ideal plants for both container gardening and for planting single plants here and there throughout your landscape.

Growing hints:

Tomatillos are extremely easy plants to grow; they need little attention during the growing season. They like to sprawl, but you can stake them or use tomato cages to save space. This plant, like tomatoes, can be pruned throughout the season as desired.

Harvesting hints:

Harvest tomatillos when the husk that surrounds the 2-inch fruit splits or turns brown and papery. The fruit is considered ripe when it is still somewhat tart; however, if you let it sit on the vine it will become sweeter.

Tomatillos will heavily self-seed the following year if ripe fruits are left on the ground after harvesting.

Journal

Variety planted:

Date planted (seeds or starts):

Location:

Date of first harvest:

Notes:

Tomatoes
Solanaceae family

Cool or warm season:	warm
Begin with:	starts
Grows as:	a bush; often needs staking, caging, or trellising
Plant size:	2'–6' tall
Plant outside:	after all chances of frost are past
Sun and location:	moderate to full sun
Soil type preferred:	well drained, high in organic matter
Planting depth:	plant with first set of leaves level with soil line
Spacing at planting:	1'–4' apart; 3'–4' between rows
Container plant:	yes, with 12" minimum soil depth, staking
Days to maturity:	from starts, 60–75
Yield per 10' row:	3/4 bushel
Harvest season:	late summer, early fall

Check farmer's markets and nurseries for unusual varieites; the flavor and variety of heirloom tomatoes can't be beat.

Suggested varieties:
Heirlooms: Cherokee Purple, Brandywine, Aunt Ruby's German Green, Kellogg's Breakfast (beefsteaks); Black Cherry (cherry).

Planting hints:
Tomatoes are ideal plants for both container gardening and planting one here or there throughout your landscape.

Tomatoes like to be planted deeply and will form new roots from the buried stem. Plant them deep enough to cover the roots and a significant portion of the stem, up to a fourth of the plant's height.

Growing hints:

Tomatoes come in two primary types: determinate and indeterminate. Determinate varieties tend to grow in a more contained fashion, and are genetically predisposed to set one crop of fruit then cease production. This is extremely useful if you are growing tomatoes for canning or want all your tomatoes to come ripe at one time.

Indeterminate varieties do the opposite—they continue to produce fruit until killed by frost. In addition, indeterminate tomato plants grow in a more dramatic sprawling manner than the determinate varieties, with their vines often reaching from 6–20 feet in length if not pruned back. Tomato cages work well for both types, but indeterminate tomatoes do best with strong central stakes or with stake-and-weave trellises (see illustration on page 30).

Harvesting hints:

Tomatoes can be picked either when they are partially or fully ripe. Heirloom varieties come in many colors, including green, orange, and purple, so judge ripeness by the fruit's softness, rather than color. Avoid pulling the fruit off the vine when harvesting—cut them instead. To encourage continued production on indeterminate varieties, pick ripe tomatoes frequently.

Journal

Variety planted:

Date planted (seeds or starts):

Location:

Date of first harvest:

Notes:

Planting, Growing, Harvesting Guide

Vegetables	March			April			May			June		
Beans							S	S	S	G	G	G
Beets				S	S	S	G	G	G	G	G	G
Brussels sprouts								S				
Carrots				S	S	S	S	S	S	G	G	G
Collards									P	G	G	G
Cucumbers										P	G	G
Edamame									S	G	G	G
Kale									P	G	G	G
Leeks									P	G	G	G
Lettuce (leaf)				S	S	S	G	G	G	H	H	H
Peas			S	G	G	G	G	G	H	H	H	
Peppers									P	G	G	G
Radish				S	S	S	G	G	G	G	G	H
Spinach				S	S	G	G	G	G	H	H	H
Squash, summer									P	G	G	G
Squash, winter									P	G	G	G
Swiss Chard						S	S	S	G	G	G	G
Tomatillos									P	G	G	G
Tomatoes									P	G	G	G

KEY: Plant Seeds: S   Plant Start: P   Growing: G   Harvest: H

note: Months are divided into early, middle, and late.

July			August			September			October			November		
G	G	G	H	H	H									
G	G	G	H	H	H	H	H	H						
	P	G	G	G	G	G	G	G	G	G	G	H	H	H
H	H	H	H	H	H	H	H	H	H	H	H			
G	G	G	H	H	H	H	H	H	H	H	H	H	H	
G	G	G	G	H	H	H	H	H						
G	G	G	G	G	G	H	H	H						
H	H	H			P	G	G	G	G	G	G		H	H
G	G	G	G	G	G									
		S	S	S	S	G	G	G	H	H	H			
	S	G	G	G	G	G	G	H	H	H				
G	G	G	H	H	H									
H	H	H												
		S	S	G	G	G	G	G	G	H	H	H		
G	G	G	H	H	H									
G	G	G	G	G	G	H	H	H						
G	H	H	S	G	G	G	G	G		H	H			
G	G	G	G	G	H	H	H	H						
G	G	G	G	G	H	H	H	H						

Chapter 5
Herbs and Edible Flowers

Herbs are not often the first thing new gardeners think about when planning their first edible garden, but they can make an enormous contribution. Herbs provide for us in many ways: adding flavor to enhance our culinary experience, providing folk remedies, and adding beauty to our lives with cut flowers, fragrances, and dyes for our clothing and artwork.

In organic gardens, herbs are used extensively as companion plants, both to attract beneficial insects and to repel destructive ones. Edible flowers also add artistry to the garden, filling in visual gaps in the garden space while we wait patiently for the vegetables to grow large and bountiful.

This chapter presents a selection of the most common and easy-to-grow herbs and edible flowers found in home gardens in the lower Great Lakes region. The list should not limit your selection, though: there are many more wonderful herbs and flowers that can easily be grown alongside your vegetables.

Basil
Lamiaceae family

Cool or warm season:	warm
Begin with:	starts
Grows as:	an annual, an individual bush
Plant size:	approx. 12"–18" tall
Plant outside:	when night temperatures stay above 55°F (13°C)
Sun and location:	full sun to part shade, needs warmth
Soil type preferred:	loose to semi-clay
Planting depth:	1/4" for seeds, root line for transplants
Spacing at planting:	1'–2' apart
Container plant:	yes, with 8" minimum soil depth
Days to maturity:	85–90
Harvest season:	mid-July through mid-September

Planting hints:

Basil is ideal for container gardening and as a border plant in formal garden spaces.

If you are lucky enough to have a sunny windowsill, don't hesitate to dig up a basil plant at the end of the season and plant it in a pot for indoor use. If your garden soil is loose and well drained, it is fine to simply dig up the plant, soil and all, and transplant directly into a pot for indoor growing. Otherwise it is best to transplant the basil to a container filled with potting mix. When late spring arrives again, you can replant the basil into the garden for a jumpstart on summer herbs.

Growing hints:

Basil can easily be damaged by excessive watering, so water just enough to keep the leaves from wilting. Basil does best when pruned frequently to encourage the production of tender young leaves and to prevent it from flowering.

Harvesting hints:
Basil can be harvested throughout the season, whenever the leaves are big enough for your needs. You can either pick individual leaves from the stems or pinch off a portion of the stem. Be careful not to strip the plant of too many of its leaves at any one time, as it needs at least half left on the plant to continue producing new leaves.

What to do with it all:
Basil leaves can be used fresh, dried or frozen.

- The fresh leaves can be left whole and added to a tossed salad, used as a colorful accent on the plate, or dropped into a jar of vinegar for flavoring.
- Used fresh, it can be made into a sauce, such as pesto.
- Dried or frozen basil is often added to tomato sauces.

Fun tidbits:
According to folklore, the scent of fresh basil evokes a sense of sympathy between two people. The juice of the basil leaf, rubbed on the skin, is said to repel mosquitoes.

Journal

Date planted (seeds or starts):

Variety or varieties planted:

Location:

Date of first harvest:

Notes:

Chamomile, German

Compositae family

Cool or warm season:	warm
Begin with:	seeds or starts
Grows as:	as an annual, a loose upright bush
Plant size:	approximately 1 1/2'–2 1/2' tall, 1' wide
Plant outside:	when night temperatures stay above 55°F (13°C)
Sun and location:	full sun to part shade
Soil type preferred:	loose to semi-clay
Planting depth:	1/4" for seeds, root line for transplants
Spacing at planting:	broadcast seeds, 1' for transplants
Container plant:	yes, with 8" minimum soil depth
Days to maturity:	70–80
Harvest season:	late summer, early fall

Planting hints:

Chamomile does extremely well when its seeds are sown directly into the garden. However, the seeds are quite small and difficult to handle individually. It's easiest to broadcast the seeds over loose soil and gently push them into the soil, or cover them with a light layer of soil.

There are two popular varieties of chamomile, German and Roman. German chamomile is an annual and grows as an upright bush; Roman chamomile is a low-growing perennial plant. German chamomile is the variety typically grown for tea.

Growing hints:

Chamomile is an easy herb to grow, and generally no special requirements or attention is required once it is established.

Harvesting hints:

The yellow center of the German chamomile flower gives chamomile tea its sour apple flavor. Pick the flowers when the white petals have started to die back and are curling under a bit.

A simple way to dry chamomile flowers is to spread them in a single layer on a paper towel. Place them indoors or outside where there is no wind, and let them air dry.

What to do with it all:

The flowers are used either fresh or dried.

- Drop a few of the fresh flowers into a cup of hot water for tea.
- Dry the flowers for later use in tea.
- Use the fresh flowers to add color to salads.

Fun tidbits:

Chamomile tea is thought to calm and soothe the nerves and is often taken before going to bed at night to help fall asleep. It is also used as a skin aid and is particularly wonderful in a foot bath.

Journal

Date planted (seeds or starts):

Variety or varieties planted:

Location:

Date of first harvest:

Notes:

Chives
Allium family

Cool or warm season:	cool
Begin with:	seeds or starts
Grows as:	perennial, a bulb with leaf stalks
Plant size:	approximately 1' tall
Plant outside:	after all danger of frost is past
Sun and location:	full sun to part shade
Soil type preferred:	loose to semi-clay
Planting depth:	1/4" for seeds, root line for transplants
Spacing at planting:	space plants 1' apart
Container plant:	yes, with 6" minimum soil depth
Days to maturity:	80
Harvest season:	spring, summer, fall

Planting Hints:

Chives spread easily in the garden if you allow the flowers to go to seed, so either carefully plan where you put this plant or be prepared to weed each spring to keep them under control.

Like basil, chives are ideal container plants. They can also be dug up in the fall and potted to grow indoors over the winter—make sure to put them in a sunny window.

Growing hints:

Chives take almost no effort to grow and are rarely affected by viruses, bugs, or four-legged creatures. Depending on the variety, chives have a mild onion or garlic flavor. They are a great alternative in the garden to onions and garlic, which are more disease prone and more difficult to grow.

Once chives become an established mass, you can easily divide them, providing you with transplants for your garden and your friends.

Harvesting hints:
All parts of this herb are edible, including the beautiful blue flowers that it produces in midsummer. To harvest the leaves, snip with scissors as close to the base as you can—this will encourage the growth of new leaves. Leave the bulbs in the ground to grow again next spring.

What to do with it all:
Chives are eaten fresh or frozen.

- Use chives wherever a delicate onion flavor is desired: in soups, salads, eggs, dips, or in hot dishes where they can be added at the end.

- Chives freeze well. Simply cut chives into small pieces (or snip with scissors), and place directly into a freezer container. Use them as you would fresh chives.

Fun tidbits:
Used extensively as a companion plant in organic gardens, chives are best known for their ability to repel aphids. Medicinally, they are thought to promote digestion and stimulate appetite.

Journal

Date planted (seeds or starts):

Variety or varieties planted:

Location:

Date of first harvest:

Notes:

Cilantro
Apiaceae / Umbelliferae family

Cool or warm season:	warm
Begin with:	seeds
Grows as:	an annual, as an individual leafy bush
Plant size:	ranges from 1 1/2'–2' tall
Plant outside:	after danger of heavy frost is past, April-June
Sun and location:	full sun
Soil type preferred:	loose to semi-clay
Planting depth:	1/2" deep
Spacing at planting:	plant 18"–24" apart
Container plant:	yes, with 8" minimum soil depth
Days to maturity:	45
Harvest season:	spring and summer

Planting Hints:

Sow cilantro seeds directly into garden beds or container soil. While you can find transplants for sale in the spring, cilantro produces a tap root and, like all plants with tap roots, they do not transplant well. Cilantro is an excellent container plant, but make sure to use a container deep enough for the tap root, ensuring a healthy and long-lasting plant.

Growing hints:

This herb tends to grow fast, setting flowers and seeds quickly, often ending its growing cycle before the summer ends.

Cilantro needs plentiful water to produce flavorful leaves; keep it well watered until it starts to bolt (suddenly flowering and setting seeds).

Harvesting hints:

Harvest cilantro leaves throughout the summer, before the plant goes to flower, picking as often as you can to encourage new growth. When harvesting cilantro, choose the smaller leaves—the larger ones tend to be bitter.

Once the plant flowers and goes to seed, gather the seeds (known as coriander) and dry them for use over the winter months. To dry the seeds, spread them on newspaper or a paper towel and place them indoors (or outdoors in a protected spot) until they are completely moisture free.

What to do with it all:

Cilantro produces both leaves and seeds that can be eaten.

- Fresh cilantro is excellent used in salsas and cucumber salads. It is used in many Mexican, Asian, and Middle Eastern dishes (see pages 123 and 131).

- Home-drying methods dull the flavor of cilantro leaves—try freezing the leaves rather than drying.

- Used whole, the seeds provide a flavor boost to wine or cider. Ground, they are used to flavor baked goods, bean dishes, sauces, soups, and other hot dishes.

Journal

Date planted (seeds or starts):

Variety or varieties planted:

Location:

Date of first harvest:

Notes:

Dill
Apiaceae / Umbelliferae family

Cool or warm season:	warm
Begin with:	seeds
Grows as:	an annual; a tall, lacy, fern-like plant
Plant size:	2'–5' tall, depending on variety
Plant outside:	late May, again every 2 weeks
Sun and location:	full sun
Soil type preferred:	loose, well drained
Planting depth:	1/2" deep
Spacing at planting:	thin seedlings to 8"–10" apart
Container plant:	yes, with 12" minimum soil depth
Days to maturity:	approximately 70
Harvest season:	summer and fall

Planting Hints:

Sow dill seeds directly into your soil. While you can find transplants for sale in the spring, dill produces a tap root, and like all plants with tap roots, it does not like to have its roots disturbed by transplanting. Dill and fennel should not be planted near each other; they will cross-pollinate, affecting the flavor of the seeds. Dill and carrots should not be planted near one another either.

There are several popular varieties of dill: Fernleaf is grown for its foliage, which is used in cooking, and Mammoth is grown for large seed heads, used in pickling.

Growing hints:

Dill is an excellent container plant, but make sure to provide it with a container deep enough for the tap root.

Harvesting hints:
Harvest the leaves throughout the summer, making sure to leave half of the plant for continued growth. Gather the seeds when the plant starts to flower. The seeds can be harvested green or after the seed heads dry and turn brown.

What to do with it all:
Both the leaves and seeds of dill are edible.

- Use the leaves, known as dill weed, either fresh or dried. Dill pairs especially well with the flavors of potatoes and cucumbers.

- The seeds can be dried for use over the winter months, or eaten right off the plant. Dill seeds are often added to soups, breads, and pickles.

- Dill leaf is easily frozen for use in winter months.

Fun tidbits:
Dill is invaluable as a replacement for salt for those on salt-restricted diets. Medicinally, chewing on dill seed can help sweeten the breath; steeped as a tea, it is said to help calm an upset stomach.

Journal

Date planted (seeds or starts):

Variety or varieties planted:

Location:

Date of first harvest:

Notes:

Fennel, Common
Umbellifer family

Cool or warm season:	warm
Begin with:	seeds
Grows as:	annual; tall lacy fern-like plant
Plant size:	3'–5' high and wide
Plant outside:	after all danger of frost is past
Sun and location:	full sun
Soil type preferred:	loose soil
Planting depth:	seeds: 1/2" deep
Spacing at planting:	2' apart
Container plant:	yes, with 12" minimum soil depth
Days to maturity:	60–70
Harvest season:	late summer

Planting hints:

Common fennel is an herb grown for its stems and seeds, in contrast to Florence fennel, which is grown for its large edible bulb.

Sow seeds directly into the soil; common fennel produces a tap root and does not like to be transplanted.

Growing hints:

Overall, fennel is quite carefree, needing little water unless drought conditions prevail. It's an excellent container plant as long as you make sure to give it enough depth for its tap root. In a container, fennel will only grow to half (about 2 feet) of the height it reaches in the garden.

Harvesting hints:

Common fennel produces edible leaves, stems, and seeds. Harvest the leaves and stems throughout the summer, making sure to leave at least half the plant for continued growth.

If you let the seeds dry on the plant, it's easiest to gather them by cutting the heads into a paper bag (mature seeds left to drop on the ground will heavily reseed the following year). Leave the seed heads in the bag to dry for a few weeks. When dried, rub the flower heads between your hands to dislodge the seeds. To prevent the aromatic oils from evaporating, store the dried seeds in an airtight glass container.

What to do with it all:

Fennel can be used fresh or dried. The seeds are delicious fresh off the plant or dried for use over the winter months.

- Use the green stems and leaves to flavor soup or chop and add to fresh salads.

- Toss dried fennel seeds into salads, soups, and salad dressings, or used crushed as a rub for meats.

Fun tidbits:

Like dill, chewing on fennel seeds can help sweeten the breath. Fennel is often used in facial steams and baths. As a facial pack, fennel tea combined with honey is reputed to reduce wrinkles.

Journal

Date planted (seeds or starts):

Variety or varieties planted:

Location:

Date of first harvest:

Notes:

Mint
Lamiaceae family

Cool or warm season:	both
Begin with:	starts or root divisions
Grows as:	a perennial
Plant size:	1/2"–24" tall
Plant outside:	any time soil is workable
Sun and location:	prefers semi-shade but full sun is okay
Soil type preferred:	loose to semi-clay
Planting depth:	soil line
Spacing at planting:	1' apart
Container plant:	yes, with 6" minimum soil depth
Days to maturity:	mature at planting
Harvest season:	spring, summer, fall

Planting hints:
Mint is very invasive, spreading by roots. A good way to keep mint from taking over is to plant it in a pot with a drainage hole in the bottom (preferably a plastic one or one that won't deteriorate from contact with soil) and sink the pot into the ground. Allow 1–2 inches of the pot to sit above the soil line. This will not only help ensure your mint won't spread into your garden (and lawn), but it will also allow you to plant more than one variety while keeping them separate.

Growing hints:
Mints are especially easy to grow. However, they do have a habit of thinning in the middle after a few years. To keep them looking neat, dig them up, remove the scraggly middle, rearrange, and replant.

Mint, like most perennials, dies back in winter. It's easy to think that the plant has died and dig up the roots, but be assured that mint is hardy in our climate and it will return in the spring.

Take a close look at the stems of your mint plants—quite unusually, they have square sides. All mint can be identified by the unique shape of its stems.

Harvesting hints:
Cut the leaves and stems as you need them, making sure to keep enough leaves on the plant for continued growth. If harvesting mint leaves for drying, pick them when the plant is just beginning to flower.

What to do with it all:
Mint leaves can be used fresh or dried.

- Chopped fresh mint leaves are a main ingredient in tabouli (see page 119) and specialty condiments.
- Fresh or dried leaves are used for teas and flavoring.

Fun tidbits:
Mint, like chives, serves to repel aphids when used as a companion plant in organic gardens. Peppermint has many medicinal uses, but it is best known for its calming effect on the stomach and for its aromatic qualities.

Journal

Date planted (seeds or starts):

Variety or varieties planted:

Location:

Date of first harvest:

Notes:

Nasturtium
Tropaeolaceae family

Cool or warm season:	cool
Begin with:	seeds
Grows as:	annuals, as either bushes or trailing vines
Plant size:	1'–2' tall bushes, 6'-8' long vines
Plant outside:	in spring when danger of heavy frost is past
Sun and location:	full to partial sun
Soil type preferred:	loose to semi-clay, well drained
Planting depth:	1/2"
Spacing at planting:	6" apart
Container plant:	yes, with 6" minimum soil depth
Days to maturity:	55-65
Harvest season:	summer through early fall

Planting hints:

Nasturtium transplants are available in the spring, but it's better to start with seeds outdoors as the plants don't like having their roots disturbed.

Ideal for container gardening and as a border plant in formal garden spaces, nasturtiums are also excellent as a secondary plant in a container with other vegetables, flowers, or herbs.

Growing hints:

This plant, while easy to grow, does have a bad habit of attracting aphids (see page 34). This pest can be managed by simply cutting off the leaves that are affected (white, raised spots on the underside of leaves are a telltale sign of aphid infestation).

On the other hand, nasturtiums can also attract beneficial insects. Often planted with squash and pumpkins, they deter squash bugs and the striped pumpkin beetle.

Harvesting hints:

Cut the flowers and leaves as desired throughout the season, making sure to keep enough leaves on the plant for continued growth (cut no more than three quarters of the plant).

What to do with it all:
The flowers, leaves, and seeds of this plant are edible.

- Fresh nasturtium flowers and leaves can be added to fresh salads wherever a mildly peppery, horseradish-like flavor is desired.

- The flowers are often used as a garnish or to add visual drama to lettuce salads.

Fun tidbits:
Nasturtiums have a unique quality: they both draw aphids away from nearby plants and they attract the hoverfly, which then goes after the aphids that have massed themselves on this beautiful plant.

The leaves are particularly high in vitamin C and iron, but only right before the plant flowers. Caution: the leaves should not be eaten in large quantities; limit intake to 1/2 oz. per day.

Journal

Date planted (seeds or starts):

Variety or varieties planted:

Location:

Date of first harvest:

Notes:

Parsley
Umbellifer family

Cool or warm season:	cool
Begin with:	starts
Grows as:	a biennial grown as an annual
Plant size:	6"–12" tall
Plant outside:	after danger of heavy frost is past, April–June
Sun and location:	partial shade
Soil type preferred:	loose to semi-clay
Planting depth:	at soil line
Spacing at planting:	1' apart
Container plant:	yes, with 6" minimum soil
Days to maturity:	mature at planting
Harvest season:	summer through fall

Planting hints:

Parsley attracts bees—where possible, plant it among fruiting vegetables that need pollination. Parsley is ideal for container gardening and as a border plant in more formal garden spaces. It is also excellent as a secondary plant in a container with other vegetables, flowers, or herbs.

Growing hints:

Parsley is easy to grow, thriving in almost any soil type. However, it doesn't like the intense heat of the summer sun, so it's best to plant it where parsley will receive light shade part of the day.

If you are lucky enough to have a sunny windowsill, don't hesitate to dig up a parsley plant at the end of the season and pot it for indoor use. Since parsley is a biennial, you can replant it into the garden in the spring for one more year of growth.

Harvesting hints:
Cut the leaves and stems as you need them throughout the season, making sure to keep at least half the leaves on the plant for continued growth.

What to do with it all:
Parsley is primarily used fresh and is often added to salads, soups and tomato sauces. It's also a main ingredient in tabouli, a traditional Middle Eastern dish (see page 119).

- Parsley is often included in traditional bouquet garnis, which are tied bundles of spices that are added to flavor soups and stews, and removed before serving.

- Home-drying methods dull the flavor of parsley. To preserve parsley, try freezing the leaves rather than drying them.

Fun tidbits:
A rich source of vitamin C, iron, and other minerals, fresh parsley is also known as an effective breath freshener. In folk medicine, chewing fresh parsley is thought to support the skin and a tea made from crushed seeds is said to kill head lice (pour the tea over the head and keep the head wrapped tightly in a towel for half an hour).

Journal

Date planted (seeds or starts):

Variety or varieties planted:

Location:

Date of first harvest:

Notes:

Sunflower
Asteraceae and Compositae family

Cool or warm season:	warm
Begin with:	seeds or starts
Grows as:	annuals
Plant size:	varies considerably; see seed packet
Plant outside:	after danger of frost is past, late May–early June
Sun and location:	full sun
Soil type preferred:	loose, well-drained
Planting depth:	1/2" deep
Spacing at planting:	3' apart
Container plant:	yes, dwarf varieties, with 12" minimum soil depth
Days to maturity:	60–75 days
Harvest season:	late summer or early fall

Planting hints:

In our climate, sunflowers germinate easily from seed, so there is rarely a need to purchase transplants. However, if you decide to grow sunflowers from starts, be aware that most of those sold in garden centers are the tall varieties.

Growing hints:

Sunflowers are easy plants to grow, and are quite tolerant of dry conditions. The taller varieties are susceptible to falling over, due to wind, animal damage, or the lack of proper root anchoring in loose soils. You may need to stake your sunflowers to keep them looking their best.

Birds also love this delicacy and you should protect the flower head if you want to harvest the seeds. The best way to do this is to tie a layer of protective fabric on the flower head before the seeds fully ripen. In a pinch you can tie on a large paper bag, but after a rain you'll have to replace the paper bag.

Harvesting hints:
Beside the seeds, the petals of the sunflower are also edible and especially pretty sprinkled in a salad. However, if you pick the petals the plant won't be able to bring its seeds to maturity. If you'd like to harvest both petals and seeds, plant enough sunflowers so you can pick petals off of some plants during the summer while leaving other plants untouched for a fall harvest of seeds.

Sunflower seeds are ready for harvesting when they move easily from side to side when you prod them with a finger.

What to do with it all:
The seeds, as well as the petals and buds, of the sunflower plant are edible.

- The seeds can be eaten raw, dried, or roasted. They're great to snack on or use in baked goods like granola, bread, and muffins.

Journal

Date planted (seeds or starts):

Variety or varieties planted:

Location:

Date of first harvest:

Notes:

Chapter 6
Putting It on the Table

Gardening is a joyful experience no matter whether you focus on flowers, fruit, vegetables, herbs, or orchards. However, growing your own vegetables and herbs is an especially wonderful experience. Along with the incomparable freshness and taste of homegrown vegetables and herbs, the satisfaction of growing your own food is hard to top.

Part of the joy of growing your own food is the astonishing variety of vegetables available, from both heirloom and hybrid seeds, some of which you may have never tried or even heard of. This chapter focuses on the vegetables and herbs featured in Chapters 4 and 5, giving basic advice on how to clean, store, and prepare each crop. In this chapter we also offer suggestions for using your harvest, more interesting facts about what you're growing, and a few recipes for enjoying the fruits of your labors.

While some crops can be harvested over a relatively long period, others will have a short burst of overwhelming productivity that is quickly over. It's worthwhile to make a plan for times of excess so your hard-won produce doesn't end up in the compost. Consider preserving a large harvest by canning or freezing, or making a much-appreciated donation to a local food pantry. Either way, you'll find immense pleasure in eating (and sharing) food from your own garden.

Cooking Techniques

With just a few basic cooking techniques, you'll find you can easily cook your produce for a delicious meal or, with simple preparation, get it ready for longer-term storage in the freezer.

Preparing vegetables for a meal

Boiling

Bring a large pan of salted water to a boil over medium-high heat. Add cleaned, cut-up vegetables to the water, bring water back to a boil and simmer (at a low boil) for the recommended time until tender. Drain and serve either hot or cold.

Steaming

Choose a pot with a tight fitting lid, large enough for a steamer insert or basket to fit inside. Place an inch or two of water in the pan, set the steamer into the pan (the water level should be just below it without touching), and bring the water to a boil over medium-high heat. Once boiling, place clean, cut-up vegetables into the basket. Cover and steam until they are done. Timing varies by vegetable, so test after color begins to brighten—they should be tender but not limp.

Roasting:

To roast vegetables, preheat oven to 375°F. Cut clean vegetables into 1–2 inch pieces. If you are using a mixture of vegetables, cut harder ones a bit smaller and softer ones a little larger, so they will be done at the same time. Place vegetables in a large mixing bowl. Add 1 or 2 tablespoons of olive oil, a teaspoon of salt, and a teaspoon of thyme or herbs of your choice. Stir to coat all pieces evenly. Spread in a single layer on one or more large, heavy-duty baking sheets. Place baking sheets in the middle of the oven. Roast 20 minutes or until vegetables begin to brown and crisp on the bottom. Remove from oven and turn pieces over. Put back in the oven until they brown on the other side, usually another 20 minutes or so. Root vegetables are especially good prepared this way.

Sautéing

Heat a tablespoon or two of oil (or butter) over medium-high heat, using a (non-stick) sauté pan or a frying pan. When the oil is hot but not smoking (butter is easily burned, so be careful it doesn't get too hot), add the vegetables all at once. Stir quickly to coat all the pieces with oil. Cook for a few minutes without stirring, until the vegetables begin to brown lightly. Occasionally stir or shake the pan to keep the vegetables from sticking. Cook until just tender.

Stir-Frying

Stir-frying is similar to sautéing but uses higher heat, requiring continuous stirring to keep the food from sticking or burning. To begin, chop your vegetables into small, bite-size pieces and separate them by the length of time they each take to cook. Using either a frying pan with straight sides or a wok, heat a few tablespoons of oil over high heat until oil is hot but not smoking. Hot oil "shimmers" when it is ready. Add vegetables to the pan in the order of cooking time needed, with the ones that take the longest time to cook added first and the ones that take the shortest time to cook added last. Once you start adding vegetables to the pan, keep them moving, stirring constantly until you turn the heat off. Another, more authentic, way to stir-fry is to cook each vegetable separately until just slightly underdone. Then, when ready to serve, stir them all together to heat and finish cooking.

Preparing vegetables for freezing

Blanching

Bring several quarts of water to a boil in a large pan so your vegetables will have plenty of room to "swim" in the water. To blanch, briefly immerse clean and cut-up vegetables in boiling water until they are slightly cooked or until their color brightens or turns bright green (usually between 1 and 4 minutes). Remove vegetables immediately, and rinse under cold water or plunge in ice water to stop the cooking. Drain well. Any water droplets will freeze into hard pieces of ice in the freezer, so make sure vegetables are just barely moist before packing into freezer containers.

Beans, Snap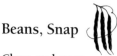

Clean and store

- Store beans in a cool, moist environment (like a re-usable plastic container) in the refrigerator after picking.

Prepare and cook

- Fresh beans are fun to eat raw in the garden, but they are especially sweet and delicious steamed until just tender and served with a little butter and salt. A quick rinse and then "topping and tailing" to snap off the ends of the beans is all that's required before cooking.

- To stir-fry, heat 1 tablespoon of olive oil in a wok or frying pan and add 1/2 lb. beans, stir-frying for 1 minute. Add 2 tablespoons of liquid, cover and steam for another minute. When liquid is gone, add 2 teaspoons of oyster sauce, soy sauce, or other liquid to pan and stir-fry just until coated.

Preserve

- Bush beans tend to produce all at once, making them an ideal variety for preserving.

- Beans freeze well and last up to a year frozen. To freeze, clean and cut to desired length, blanch quickly in boiling water—until bright green—then drain, cool under a stream of cold water, and drain again. Pack beans in any freezer-appropriate container.

Did you know?

- Beans have been cultivated in the Americas for over 6,000 years. Squash, corn, and beans grown together comprise the traditional "Three Sisters Garden," a mutually beneficial companion planting used by indigenous Americans since pre-historic times.

- More than 130 varieties of snap beans (eaten in the pod) are known. They come in many colors: green, yellow, purple, red, or streaked. Snap beans can be thin like the French haricot "fillet" varieties, or wide, like the broad "Romano" varieties, or up to 18 inches long like the Chinese "yard-long bean" or "asparagus bean."

- The flowers of all beans are edible; use them freely as an attractive garnish.

Beets

Clean and store

- Clean beets by first rinsing off garden dirt. Store in a cool, moist environment.

- Beet greens are edible and good for you. Clean greens by soaking in a large tub of clean water. Drain and repeat until water is free from debris. Remove stems if you wish.

Prepare and cook

- Beets are wonderful eaten raw. Try grating a peeled beet to add to a cabbage-based slaw for color and added nutrition.

- When ready to use for a meal, trim greens to within 1 inch of the root (do not cut into the root itself, to prevent excessive bleeding). Scrub beet roots with a vegetable brush before cooking or peeling.

- Oven roast whole beets in foil, or boil clean but unpeeled beets until tender. Once the beets cool slightly, the skins can be rubbed off or peeled easily with a knife. Cooked beets can be eaten hot as a side dish or cold as a colorful addition to a salad.

- Sauté beet greens until tender in a little olive oil with a few cloves of garlic. Add a bit of salt and enjoy. Or, use as you would any sturdy green—they are especially good with pasta and white beans.

Preserve

- A delicious way to preserve beets is to can old-fashioned spicy, pickled beets.

- Extended storage for beets is possible through the winter months if kept in a cool indoor space and packed in paper, sand, or sterile soil. When preparing for storage, manually knock off any large clumps of soil, but do not wash them or cut off the tail of the root. Cut off the greens, leaving a good inch of the stem.

Did you know?

- Beets have been cultivated since 800 BC. The earliest cultivars were black or white rather than red.

- The rich color of beets indicates their extraordinary nutritional value.

- The Detroit Dark Red Beet is a very popular heirloom variety, first established in the 1890s. It's a large, sweet, prolific variety well-adapted to a northern or Great Lakes climate.

- Beets now come in red, white, golden, and a pink-and-white striped variety known as Chioggia.

- Sugar beets produce 30 percent of the world's sugar. Sebewaing, Michigan is called the sugar beet capital of the world.

Roasted Beets

1 lb beets (approximately 4 small)

1/4 cup water

3 TB olive oil

1 TB wine or rice vinegar

1 tsp lemon juice

1/2 tsp salt

Pinch of black pepper

1/4 cup thin slivers of red onion

2 TB finely chopped fresh dill

Preheat the oven to 375°F. Trim the greens from the beets, leaving about 1/4 inch. Place the beets in a baking dish with the water and cover (use foil if the dish doesn't have a lid). Bake until the beets are tender when pierced with a knife, about 1 hour. Cool slightly. Slip the skins off the beets by gently rubbing them with your fingers. Cut into 1/4-inch thick slices.

In a large bowl, whisk together the vinegar, lemon juice, olive oil, and salt and pepper. Add the beets and onions and toss gently to coat. Stir in the dill and serve.

Brussels sprouts

Clean and store
- Store brussels sprouts in the coldest part of your refrigerator. They keep best (up to six weeks) at near-freezing temperatures.
- Clean brussels sprouts for cooking by rinsing in clear water. Trim off the base of the sprout along with any loose or ragged leaves.

Prepare and cook
- Brussels sprouts are especially well suited to sautéing and roasting. They can be cooked whole, halved, shaved into thin slices, or separated into individual leaves.
- Try cutting sprouts in half, browning well in olive oil (or bacon fat), and then braising in cream until tender. Add salt and pepper. This method creates brussels sprouts converts.
- Brussels sprouts will release an unpleasant sulphur smell if overcooked or boiled too long.

Preserve
- Brussels sprouts freeze well. To freeze, blanch quickly in boiling water just until bright green, then drain and cool under a stream of cold water. Pack in an appropriate freezer container.

Did you know?
- Brussels sprouts are closely related to the cabbages they resemble; they originated in Belgium around the 1600s, as a dwarf or mutant cultivar of the Savoy cabbage.
- They came to the U.S. in the early 1800s, where the satirist Mark Twain joked that "to eat brussels sprouts is to deprive cabbage of their young."
- One cup of cooked Brussels sprouts contains 810 units of vitamin A, 423 milligrams of potassium, and 112 milligrams of phosphorous—an enormous amount! In addition, this same cup also contains significant amounts of thiamine, riboflavin, and ascorbic acid.

Carrots

Clean and store

- To store carrots, clean dirt from the root and remove the leafy green tops. Keep in a cool, moist environment. Do not peel carrots before storing.

- Carrots can be stored for extended periods in a cool indoor area or root cellar by packing them in paper, sand, or sterile soil.

Prepare and cook

- Although most people seem to be habituated to it, carrots do not need peeling—just scrub with a vegetable brush and save valuable nutrition and fiber from the compost heap.

- Grated, raw carrots add color and vitamins to salads, stir-fries, casseroles, soups, or vegetable pancakes. Grated raw carrots also add a moist sweetness that is delicious in baked goods like carrot cake or carrot muffins.

- Roast or steam carrots, cut in any length or shape desired, just until tender for a delicious and colorful side dish. Sprinkle with brown sugar and butter for a treat.

Preserve

- Try Spicy Pickled Carrots for a tongue-tingling side dish for Mexican meals. Blanch 4 cups of carrots into 3-inch lengths, drain, and place carrots in clean pint jars. In a small pot, boil 1 cup cider or rice vinegar, 1 cup water and 1 tablespoon pickling spice for 5 minutes. Pour over carrots, cool, and refrigerate.

Did you know?

- The earliest reference to carrots comes from ancient Babylonia (now Iraq), where they were originally grown for their edible leaves and seeds.

- The purple root of the early carrot plant was not considered edible. Sweet orange carrots are believed to have originated as an improved variety coming from the Andalusia region of Spain.

- The longest carrot ever recorded was nearly 17 feet; the heaviest weighed almost 19 pounds.

- Carrots were the first vegetable to be canned commercially.

Collard greens

Clean and store

- Store collard greens in a very cold (nearly freezing is best), moist environment.

- Rinse collard greens before using.

Prepare and cook

- Collard greens, also known simply as collards, have a tough central rib that should be removed before cooking.

- Collard greens have thick and substantial leaves. They are often used in combination with, and can be substituted for, other substantial greens like kale in casseroles, pasta, or soups.

- Typical preparations of collards call for extended cooking time in a broth (which also becomes part of the meal). However, collard greens can also be thinly sliced and quickly sauteed (try them with garlic) to preserve more of their color and flavor.

Preserve

- Cooked collard greens can be kept for over a week in the refrigerator or for several months stored in the freezer.

Did you know?

- Collard greens are a staple vegetable in the American South, where they are traditionally cooked with smoked and salted meats, diced onion, vinegar, and pepper in plenty of liquid. Cornbread is often served with collards to soak up the juices known as "pot likker."

- In some cultures, collard greens are eaten on New Year's Day with black-eyed peas and cornbread. These greens resemble folded money and are thought to ensure wealth for the coming year.

- Collard greens can be thinly sliced, salted, and fermented to make "collard kraut."

Cucumbers

Clean and store

- Store cucumbers in a cool environment. When stored in a closed plastic bag or container, the accumulation of excess water can turn cucumbers slimy. Make sure they have some air circulation.

- Wash cucumbers and remove any spines just before using.

Prepare and cook

- Usually small, firm cucumbers are the sweetest. If your cucumbers are on the bitter side, try cutting off a large section of the stem end and, in addition to removing the green peel, remove a significant layer of the white flesh.

- The peel of the cucumber is edible, though it can sometimes be tough and somewhat bitter on mature fruits.

- To make your cucumbers "burpless," cut them in half lengthwise and use a spoon to scoop out the seeds.

- Salt cucumber slices and allow them to drain to emphasize their crunchiness.

- For an old-fashioned summertime side dish, combine thinly sliced cucumbers with a few spoonfuls of sour cream, some thinly sliced onion, salt and pepper.

- Cucumbers are good raw in salads or on a vegetable tray, but they are members of the squash family and can also be served cooked as a side dish or pureed in soups.

Preserve

- The main method for preserving cucumbers is pickling. There are thousands of recipes, from sweet and spicy to sour and garlicky. Making refrigerator pickles is a quick and easy way to get some good pickle flavor without canning.

Did you know?

- Cucumbers have been grown for more than 3,000 years, starting in Western Asia. They were grown in France starting in the 9th century, in England in the 14th century, and in the U.S. in the 16th century.

- Early American cookbooks suggest braising cucumbers and then baking them in cream.

Refrigerator Dill Pickles

12 small (3"–4") pickling cucumbers

2 cups water

1 3/4 cups vinegar (distilled, wine, cider or rice)

1 1/2 cups chopped dill weed

1/4 cup sugar

8 cloves garlic, chopped

1 1/2 TB Kosher salt

1 TB pickling spice

1/2 tsp dried crushed red pepper

4 sprigs fresh dill weed

Combine all ingredients except dill sprigs in a large bowl. Stir, let stand at room temperature for 2 hours until sugar and salt dissolve.

Put 4 cucumbers into each 1 1/2-pint wide-mouth jar. Tuck a sprig of fresh dill among the cucumbers in each jar. Ladle pickling liquid from the bowl to cover cucumbers, and seal jars with lids. Refrigerate at least 10 days before eating. Pickles will stay fresh for up to 1 month (keep refrigerated).

Edamame

Clean and store

- Edamame are also known as "green soybeans" because they are picked before they ripen into dried beans. Store edamame in the pod in the refrigerator.

- Rinse off any accumulated dirt before cooking.

Prepare and cook

- Edamame are usually cooked by boiling or steaming in the pod, though the pod is not edible. Edamame can be eaten as a snack or appetizer, served in the pod, or they can also be used, shelled, in place of lima beans or fava beans.

- Prepare a pot of boiling, salted water. Cook edamame until tender, about 4 minutes. Cool. Serve edamame in the pod by squeezing the pod with your fingers until the bean pops into your mouth.

Preserve

- Edamame freeze well and last up to a year frozen. To freeze, blanch pods quickly in boiling water until bright green, then drain and cool under a stream of cold water. Pack in any freezer-appropriate container.

Did you know?

- Edamame are known as "maodou" (meaning "hairy bean") in China, where they have been grown for more than 2,200 years.

- Some edamame varieties have very unusual names: one is called "Beer Friend," another "Envy," and another "Green Pearls."

Kale

Clean and store

- Kale loves the cold; store, unwashed, in the coldest part of the refrigerator in a plastic bag or re-usable container.

- When ready to use, wash kale leaves in a big tub of clean water. Drain and repeat until water is free from debris.

Prepare and cook

- Kale usually has a tough central rib. If you wish, remove this before cooking.

- There are many varieties of kale, each with a slightly different texture and flavor, but any can easily substitute for another. In general, kale is a hearty green that stands up well to longer cooking in casseroles and soups but can also be cooked more quickly in sautéed or stir-fried dishes.

- Shred kale and sauté with olive oil and garlic for a tasty side dish.

- "Kale Chips" are an especially good way to serve kale to children and those new to this vegetable.

Preserve
- Freeze kale leaves by cleaning and putting them directly into the freezer in a freezer bag. Freezing this way breaks down some of their toughness. The kale can be thawed to use in casseroles, soups, or pasta dishes.

Did you know?
- Dieticians and scientists consider kale, a member of the cabbage family, to be among the most nutritious of all vegetables, with powerful anti-oxidant, anti-inflammatory, and anti-cancer properties.

- During World War II, the British government encouraged citizens to plant kale because it is especially easy to grow, tolerant of many soil conditions, and provided many nutrients that had been removed from the regular diet by rationing.

Kale Chips

4 cups firmly-packed kale

1 TB extra-virgin olive oil

1 tsp tamari or other soy sauce

Preheat oven to 375°F. Wash and trim the kale: remove the tough stems by folding the kale leaves in half and cutting out the stem. Tear each leaf into hand-size pieces. Toss with extra-virgin olive oil and tamari.

Place kale on a cookie sheet and roast for 5 minutes. Turn over and roast another 5–10 minutes, until just crispy and beginning to turn faintly brown. Remove from oven and serve immediately. 2–4 servings.

Leeks

Clean and store

- Although they have the flavor of onions (and, indeed, are members of the onion family), leeks are milder than either regular cooking onions or green onions. The white root and tender pale green part of the leek are the edible parts. The tough, dark-green leaves can be used to make soup stock.

- Leeks can be harvested long into the season, and they store well (up to 2 weeks) refrigerated in a plastic bag to retain moisture.

- Leeks often hide sandy grit inside their many layers. To clean a leek, remove the very end of the root and the tough, dark-green leaves. Cut the remaining leek in half lengthwise and run under cool water, making sure the water runs over each layer.

Prepare and cook

- Cooked, leeks can replace onions in most dishes (although stronger-flavored onions won't necessarily be able to replace leeks in the reverse situation). Leeks can be also be served thinly sliced, raw, in a salad.

- Make a side dish of leeks to serve as a topping for fish or hamburgers, or as an appetizer on top of toasted slices of French bread with goat cheese. Thinly slice 4–5 cleaned leeks, then, over medium-low heat, sauté slices in 4–5 tablespoons of melted butter or olive oil until tender and beginning to brown (about 25 minutes). Add a pinch of sugar to aid the caramelization. Add a pinch of salt, also.

Preserve

- Preserve cleaned leeks by blanching in boiling water 2–3 minutes, then freeze in an appropriate container or freezer bag. The leeks will lose some texture and flavor, but will still work well in cooked dishes.

Did you know?

- The cold, creamy potato-leek soup known as vichyssoise, likely the most well-known leek dish in the U.S., sounds French, but was actually invented at the Ritz Carlton Hotel in New York around 1900.

- The leek is the national symbol of Wales, recalling a 7th century battle in which the Welsh defeated the Saxons. In that battle, which took place in a leek field, the Welsh wore leeks fixed to their helmets to differentiate themselves from their opponents. The leek emblem is still used as a cap badge of the Welsh Guards.

~~~~~~~~~~

Tabouli

1/2 cup quinoa or bulgur

3 TB olive oil

1 cup finely chopped, fresh flat-leaf parsley (from 3 bunches)

1/2 cup finely chopped fresh mint

1/2 cup minced leeks (white stalks and green stems)

2 medium tomatoes, diced into 1/4" pieces (or 2 cups cherry tomatoes, halved)

1/4 cup fresh lemon juice

1/2 tsp salt

pinch of black pepper (optional)

This recipe is great with either quinoa or bulgur. To cook quinoa, bring it to a boil in a pot with 2 quarts of water. Simmer until tender, 10–15 minutes. Drain. For bulgur, stir together bulgur and 1 tablespoon of the olive oil in a heatproof bowl. Add 1 cup boiling water, then cover bowl tightly and let stand 45 minutes. Drain in a sieve, pressing slightly to remove excess liquid.

Transfer quinoa or bulgur to a bowl and toss with remaining ingredients, until combined well. Serve chilled or at room temperature.

Lettuce

Clean and store

- Freshly picked leaf lettuces are delicate and very perishable. Eat them as soon as possible after harvesting. One technique to help with this is to clean lettuces immediately and store in the refrigerator, ready for a sandwich or quick salad.

- Clean freshly picked lettuces by putting the leaves in a large tub of clean water. Swish gently so dirt and sand will fall to the bottom of the tub. Remove lettuce, drain dirty water and repeat with clean water until water is free from debris.

- Once they are clean, drain lettuce leaves, then dry them in a salad spinner or with a clean towel until they are just barely damp. Store in a cool, moist environment, but not in the coldest part of the refrigerator. Lettuce leaves freeze easily.

Prepare and cook

- Chefs prefer to tear lettuce leaves rather than cut them with a knife. Cutting lettuce leaves with a knife is thought to make them "bleed," or turn brown around the edges.

- Gather a beautiful salad from your garden made from lettuce leaves, tiny bits of tender herbs, and edible flowers like sunflowers or nasturtiums. Focus attention on it as a refreshing, appetite-stimulating first course by tossing with a simple vinaigrette of vinegar and olive oil, with a pinch of dry mustard, salt, and pepper.

Preserve

- Because the leaves are so delicate, lettuce must be quickly consumed and is not appropriate for canning, freezing, or drying.

Did you know?

- There are hundreds, if not thousands, of varieties of lettuce cultivars. In China, lettuces are divided into "leaf-use" varieties and "stem-use" varieties. Robust, thick-stemmed varieties of bitter lettuces are preferred for stir-frying and stewing.

- In France, the salad course is typically eaten after the main dish and before the cheese or dessert course.

Peas

Clean and store

- Peas come in two varieties with either edible (sometimes called snap, sugar, or snow peas) or non-edible pods (sometimes called shelling or "English" peas). The edible-pod types are harvested before the peas inside develop, while those with non-edible pods are harvested once the peas inside fill out. Both should be stored in a covered container in the refrigerator until ready for use.

- Shelling peas will be sweeter if stored in the pod in the refrigerator until ready to cook. The sugar content of shelling peas is quickly turned to starch when stored, so eat them as soon as possible for maximum sweetness.

Prepare and cook

- In general, both types of peas have a "string" along the top spine that should be removed along with the ends before cooking and eating. To string a pea, simply pull the stem end downward and tear off the string that follows.

- Remove English or shelling peas from the pod before cooking.

- Picking and eating peas raw from the vine is a nice treat as you walk through your garden.

- Peas can be quickly blanched, cooled, and added to cold salads or other dishes.

- Creamed peas and new potatoes is one of the first and most delicious treats of late spring and early summer. To make, first scrub new potatoes, but don't peel them. If larger than a golf ball, cut into quarters. Steam until just tender. While the potatoes are cooking, briefly boil fresh peas until barely cooked, 1–2 minutes. Drain. When potatoes are tender, drain, then add the peas. Heat gently with enough cream to coat the peas and potatoes. Add salt and pepper.

Preserve

- Peas are easily frozen. Blanch in boiling water until bright green, rinse in cold water to stop the cooking process, drain well, and pack in meal-sized freezing containers.

Did you know?

- Peas, introduced in the 1700s in England and France, were wildly popular and eating them was "both a fashion and a madness."

- In the early 1880s, the Austrian monk, Gregor Mendel, used peas to demonstrate that certain traits were inherited from parent to child. His work became the foundation of the study of genetics.

Peppers

Clean and store

- Peppers generally come from the garden without much dirt. Store in the vegetable drawer of the refrigerator and give a quick rinse when ready to use.

Prepare and cook

- Hot peppers can be quite painful to the skin, eyes, and mucus membranes. The hottest parts of peppers are the veins and the seeds. When handling hot peppers, wear rubber or latex gloves. If handling hot peppers without gloves, be sure to wash your hands with soap immediately afterward.

- Yellow and orange peppers are generally the sweetest and can be interchanged with sweet red peppers. Green bell peppers are not quite as sweet (they are the unripe fruit of a sweet red pepper), but are also delicious and often used in savory dishes, like chili or stuffed peppers. All sweet peppers are good sliced into strips to eat raw or added to a salad.

- Prepare sweet peppers by cutting in half and removing the core of small white seeds inside. Rinse out any seeds that stick inside.

- Cook sweet peppers alongside potatoes, carrots, onions, brussels sprouts, and other vegetables tossed with olive oil and thyme. Bake in the oven until caramelized and tender for an excellent side dish.

- Roasting peppers concentrates their sweetness. To roast on the grill or under the broiler, cut peppers in half and remove seeds. With skin toward heat source, cook until well-charred. Cool, and the blackened skin should slip off easily. Roasted pepper slices are delicious on pizza or in a sandwich with goat cheese.

- Cut roasted peppers in 1-inch pieces and marinate in olive oil with several cloves of sliced garlic. Serve on slices of baguette for a great appetizer.

Preserve
- Raw peppers will become mushy in the freezer, but roasted sweet peppers can be packaged and frozen in small amounts to add summery flavor to wintertime dishes.

Did you know?
- Sweet peppers can be white, purple, blue, or even brown.
- Planting peppers throughout the garden helps deter viruses.

Mild Salsa

1 1/2 pounds tomatoes, seeded and diced

1 small onion, finely chopped

1–2 jalapeño chile peppers, seeded and finely chopped

2 TB chopped fresh cilantro

2 TB fresh lime juice

3/4 tsp salt

Tomato prep (optional): To remove skins, place tomatoes in boiling water for 1 minute, then plunge them into ice water—the skins will peel off easily.

With sharp knife, cut tomatoes into quarters and use a fingertip to remove seeds and pulp. Chop tomato sections into 1/2-inch pieces. Combine tomato, onion, jalapeño, cilantro, lime juice, and salt in medium-size bowl. For best flavor, refrigerate, covered, for a few hours or overnight.

Radishes

Clean and store
- Rinse, if they are very dirty, and store radishes with the leaves still on in a cool, moist environment.

Prepare and cook
- All parts of the radish are edible, including the leaves. Both roots and leaves can be eaten raw or cooked. To prepare, remove leaves and scrub the radish root with a vegetable brush under cold water.

- Radishes are typically eaten raw and unpeeled, but they can be served cooked. Try serving roasted or sauteed radishes as a side dish.

- Chopped radishes add a splash of bright color and spicy flavor to a cold salad. Grated, they can be used as the main ingredient in a slaw recipe.

- Left whole or sliced in half, radishes can be eaten as a snack, with a dip or without.

- Many people enjoy radish sandwiches: spread fresh bread with butter or olive oil, top with a layer of thinly sliced radishes. Add salt and pepper. Enjoy.

Preserve
- In many Asian countries, radishes—especially the long, white daikon radish—are preserved by pickling.

Did you know?
- Radish plants grown among cucumbers deter cucumber beetles.

- There are many varieties of radishes and they come in a rainbow of colors, including red, white, pink, purple, and black.

- Round radishes can vary from the size of a cherry to the size of a basketball; for the long ones, the size can be as tiny as a pinkie finger or as long and as thick as an arm.

- Some radishes are grown specifically for their leaves, some for their seeds, and some for the oil of their seeds, rather than for the radish root.

Spinach

Clean and store

- Clean spinach as you would other leafy greens—remove any tough stems and submerge leaves in a large tub of clean water. After rinsing, remove leaves, drain dirty water, and repeat until water is free from sand and debris.
- Dry spinach in a salad spinner and store in a clean plastic bag in the refrigerator.

Prepare and cook

- Spinach can be eaten either cooked or fresh. Shredded or torn spinach leaves are wonderful salad greens on their own or a great addition to fresh lettuce leaves as the base of a salad.
- Cooked spinach can be used as a side dish—try it sautéed with olive oil and a few cloves of minced garlic or sliced onions. It can also be added to soups and quiches, or it can be made into fillings for spinach pie, enchiladas, or crepes.
- Before adding cooked spinach to a dish, be sure to press out and drain any liquid. Otherwise, your dish will be too watery.

Preserve

- Cooked spinach can easily be frozen. Steam it until just wilted, press out and drain any liquid, then freeze the spinach in an appropriate container.

Did you know?

- Although it has become known in modern times as a popular vegetable of the Mediterranean, the earliest varieties of spinach grew in Persia (now Iran) and southwest Asia. In 647 AD, spinach was taken from Nepal to China, where it is still known as the "Persian green."
- Although spinach is a good source of iron, that iron only becomes available for our bodies to use if spinach is eaten together with a source of vitamin C (like oranges or tomatoes).

Summer Squash: Zucchini, Yellow, etc.

Clean and store
- Store summer squash in the refrigerator in a cool and moist, but not wet, environment, such as an open plastic bag.
- Rinse any dirt from summer squash before using.

Prepare and cook
- Cut stem and blossom ends off squash and then slice to prepare. Summer squash does not need to be peeled.
- Although mostly eaten cooked, tender-skinned summer squash can be eaten raw. Try paper-thin slices of raw zucchini "carpaccio" with a mint and citrus marinade, or use paper-thin slices of summer squash as a replacement for noodles in a pasta salad.
- Sliced summer squash is a tasty, simple side dish when sautéed or stir fried with onions and herbs, .
  - Grilling is a wonderful and easy way to cook summer squash. Slice squash in lengthwise strips about 1/2-inch thick. Brush with oil, sprinkle with salt and pepper, and place on the grill, cut side down. Turn when partially cooked and continue until done—about 6–10 minutes total, depending on how hot the grill is.
- Summer squash is also delicious stuffed. Slice squash in half lengthwise and scoop out the pulp to make a "canoe." Mix pulp with additional ingredients such as cheese, herbs, onion, meat, vegetables, rice, or bread crumbs. Add stuffing back into the "canoe" and bake at 350°F until squash is tender, about 45 minutes.

Preserve
- Summer squash can be grated and frozen for later use in zucchini bread.

Did you know?
- The flower of the squash plant is edible. This delicacy is often served stuffed, or battered and fried. Try sautéing squash blossoms in a little bit of butter or olive oil until wilted. Add a sprinkle of salt. This is a wonderful garnish or appetizer.
- The English word "squash" comes from the Narragansett word "askutasquash," meaning "a green thing eaten raw."

Winter Squash: Acorn, Butternut, Hubbard, Spaghetti, etc.

Clean and store
- Brush away any dirt and store hard-skinned winter squash in a cool, dark place with plenty of air circulation.

Prepare and cook
- The simplest method for cooking is to cut winter squash in half lengthwise carefully with a large knife. Scoop out the seeds and any stringy bits with a large spoon, then place both halves, cut-side down, on an oiled baking sheet. Bake at 350°F until tender. Depending on the size of the squash, baking can take from 30 minutes to over an hour. Allow squash to cool enough to scoop out the flesh. To serve, sprinkle with salt and pepper or mix with butter, and brown sugar or maple sugar.

- Purée cooked squash to add to soups; use in muffins, pancakes, or other quick breads; or make into a delicious filling for ravioli or enchiladas.

- Winter squash is also a great addition to a roasted vegetable mix. Cut squash in half, remove seeds, and peel carefully. Then cut squash into bite-size cubes and add to other cut-up vegetables (like potatoes, cauliflower, brussels sprouts, peppers, onion, etc.) and coat with a tablespoon or two of olive oil. Add a teaspoon of thyme and a teaspoon of salt. Mix well. Spread in a single layer on a heavy-duty baking sheet. Roast at 375°F for 20 minutes, remove from oven and stir. Roast for another 20–30 minutes, until vegetables are tender and have some crusty brown bits.

Preserve
- Fully ripe, unbruised winter squash will keep several months through the winter if properly stored in a cool—below 65°F (18°C)—but not freezing, dark, airy place.

- Winter squash can also be preserved by putting cooked, puréed squash into the freezer in meal-sized serving containers.

Did you know?
- Winter squash is native to North America and is thought to have originated in northern Argentina near the Andes mountains.

- Squash seeds (the part inside the seed case) are edible. Try them roasted and salted or ground into a paste. The shoots, leaves, and tendrils of squash are also edible as cooked greens.

- Green- and yellow-striped Delicata squash is also called "sweet potato squash"; it was developed to be a substitute for sweet potatoes in regions (like the Dakotas) unsuited to the cultivation of regular sweet potatoes.

Swiss Chard

Clean and store

- Swiss chard should be stored immediately in the refrigerator in a plastic bag to avoid wilting.

- To clean Swiss chard, submerge leaves in a large tub of clean water. Agitate gently, then remove chard, drain water, and repeat until the water is free from debris.

Prepare and cook

- Swiss chard is frequently eaten as two separate vegetables—the stalks are used like celery and the leaf used as a green. If eaten together, the stalks need more cooking time and so should be cooked for a few minutes first and the leaves added later.

- The leaves can be treated like (and mixed with) any of the heartier greens or spinach. Swiss chard is very good sautéed in olive oil with either sliced garlic or sliced onions.

- Cooked, Swiss chard can be used as a side dish on its own, or in soups, quiches, casseroles, and in various fillings for spinach pie, ravioli, or crepes.

Preserve

- Swiss chard can be cooked, pureed and frozen, but is not generally considered a good candidate for preserving.

Did you know?

- Swiss chard can be left in the garden all winter. It will sprout new leaves once spring arrives, providing an early-season green.

- An old-fashioned name for Swiss chard is Silverbeet. It was considered a "rootless" beet variety.

Tomatillos

Clean and store

- After removing the husks, wash tomatillos. They are often sticky.

- Keep ripe tomatillos in the refrigerator. They will keep longer if the husks are removed and the fruits are stored in sealed plastic bags.

Prepare and cook

- Tomatillos are prized in Mexican and other Latin American dishes for their fresh green color and tart flavor. They can be eaten raw or cooked.

- To make salsa verde, a traditional green sauce used in Mexican dishes, roast tomatillos, onion, tomato, and garlic under the broiler or in a dry skillet until slightly charred. Cool and puree with a handful of cilantro.

Preserve

- Freeze tomatillos whole or cut in slices.

Did you know?

- Tomatillos are usually eaten green, but when ripe they can be green, yellow, purple, or red.

- To produce fruit, two or more tomatillo plants are needed for pollination.

Tomatoes

Clean and store

- A quick rinse is usually all that's needed to clean tomatoes.

- Do not store tomatoes in the refrigerator; the cold will turn them mealy. Instead, store them in a colander or in a basket on the countertop. They do best with some air circulation.

Prepare and cook

- Use summer-ripe tomatoes in ways that highlight their superior taste, color, and texture; for example, as a main ingredient in a bread salad, as the base for a cold soup, or as the "T" in a BLT.

- To peel tomatoes, place them in boiling water for 1 minute, then plunge them into a bowl of ice water. The skins will split slightly and peel easily. If you want to remove the seeds, cut the peeled tomato into quarters and remove the seeds from the sections with your fingertip.

- One of the best ways to use summertime tomatoes is in gazpacho. Peel and puree tomatoes, add a clove or two of minced garlic and a tablespoon or two of olive oil and red wine or cider vinegar. Add finely chopped cucumber, green or red pepper, onion, and cilantro or parsley. Serve with toasted bread.

- Marinara sauce is an Italian staple for pasta. To 2 tablespoons of olive oil, add 2–3 chopped cloves of garlic and cook over low heat in a frying pan. Dice 6 peeled and seeded tomatoes, and add to the pan, cooking for 20 minutes. Add 6–10 ripped basil leaves and cook for another minute. Serve over pasta and top with freshly grated Parmesan cheese.

- Fried green tomatoes, popular throughout the American South, are easy to make. Dip 1/4-inch slices of green tomatoes in buttermilk, then coat with either cornmeal, bread crumbs or seasoned flour. Fry in hot oil until browned, about 3 minutes. Flip, brown the other side, add salt and pepper, and serve.

Preserve

- At the end of the season, green tomatoes with even the faintest bit of color can ripen if stored in a dark, cool, dry place. Wrap them in clean paper and store in a single layer to prevent bruising. Check every few days to see which tomatoes are ripening and discard any that start to go bad.

- Ripe tomatoes are excellent candidates for almost all preservation methods: drying, canning, freezing, and pickling. Consider ways to use up green tomatoes, too, like green tomato mincemeat, chow-chow pickles, green tomato chutney, or green tomato conserve.

- Sun-dried or oven-dried tomatoes have sweet, very concentrated tomato flavor. Any variety can be used, but large quantities of small or plum varieties work best. To dry tomatoes, remove core, cut in half lengthwise, and arrange cut-side up on a heavy baking sheet lined with parchment. Sprinkle with salt, pepper, garlic, herbs, and olive oil. Roast in a slow oven (250°F) for several hours, until tomatoes have shriveled to the desired consistency. Once done, pack tomatoes in olive oil to store in the refrigerator or freeze them in meal-sized quantities in small, plastic freezer bags.

Did you know?

- Tomatoes were cultivated in southern Mexico by 500 BC. They are native to the Americas and originated from the west coast of South America.

- Popular heirloom tomato varieties include Brandywine, Green Zebra, and Purple Cherokee.

Tomato, Basil and Mozzarella Salad

Two large tomatoes

10 large, fresh basil leaves

1/2 lb. fresh mozzarella cheese

2 TB olive oil

Salt and pepper to taste

Slice the tomatoes and mozzarella cheese into 1/4-inch slices, and chop or slice the basil into thin strips. On a plate, arrange the tomato slices alternately with mozzarella and top with the basil.

Drizzle the salad with olive oil and add salt and pepper to taste.

Chapter 7

Challenging Edibles

Some of the most delightful edibles are often frustrating for new gardeners. The reasons for this vary from growing requirements to pollination needs to susceptibility to disease. Each of the plants in this chapter has both challenges and great appeal. After reading through this chapter, you may choose to avoid these plants in your first few seasons. If, however, you want to be adventurous and try your hand at a few of them, I invite you to find out more from your local Extension office, online sources, or your local library. Seeking out local references will alert you to any information specific to your region—for example, which varieties might be most successful.

Perhaps the most challenging of the crops in this chapter are strawberries. First-time gardeners are often drawn to growing strawberries—who can resist their delicious fruit? However, strawberries are one of the more failure-prone plants in the garden for new gardeners, and thus they are worthy of a strong word of warning.

Corn (*Gramineae family*)

Why this plant is challenging:
disease prone, pollination requirements

- Corn has a tendency to be attacked by corn smut, a fungal disease that is difficult to control. Unfortunately, corn smut does not appear until the cob has formed and you are anticipating harvesting your crop. This unexpected development, coming so late in the growing cycle, can be discouraging to new gardeners.

- Wind pollinated, corn must be grown close enough to other corn for tassels to touch when blown by the wind. This requires planting corn in large groupings, rather than in single rows or sparingly. This requirement must be strictly adhered to for cobs to form without having to be pollinated by hand.

Why gardeners like to grow this plant:
fun, variety

- Corn is a dramatic plant—it grows rapidly and, depending on the variety, it can grow extremely tall. Children find this plant extremely fun to watch grow, rating right up there with sunflowers.

- A number of wonderful varieties that are not available in grocery stores can be grown in home gardens.

- For those who love corn, the taste of freshly picked corn from the garden can't be beat.

Eggplant (*Solanaceae family*)

Why this plant is challenging:
disease prone, time consuming

- Eggplant has a tendency to attract mites, aphids, and mildews, making it difficult even for seasoned gardeners to maintain the health of this plant without significant effort.

- To ensure the plant bushes out, the tip of the plant must be pinched off when it reaches 12 inches tall.

- Eggplant needs a regular application of fertilizer.

Why gardeners like to grow this plant:

unusual varieties, adaptability

- There are a number of wonderful heirloom varieties available if you are willing to start this plant from seed.

- Eggplant does not need, or even like, full sun; thus, this plant can be grown in otherwise unused spaces in the garden.

- This vegetable grows extremely well in a container.

Garlic *(Allium family)*

Why this plant is challenging:

requirements for growing

- Garlic requires a loose soil in order to form a nicely shaped bulb.

- Figuring out when to plant garlic can be tricky, due to seasonal weather fluctuations. It is usually planted around November 1.

- Garlic needs to be watered, fertilized, and weeded throughout the spring.

- If you grow garlic to store over the winter, you will need to let it dry thoroughly before storing, or it will quickly rot.

Why gardeners like to grow this plant:

economy of growing for winter storage

- If properly dried and stored, garlic makes a great crop for winter storage.

- Garlic is an interesting plant to grow and you can plant a large quantity in a small space. In mass, it makes a pleasing sight.

- In the spring, the green leaves can be harvested and used as you would chives.

Onion *(Allium family)*

Why this plant is challenging:

requirements for growing, disease prone

- Onions require a loose soil in order to form a large, ball-shaped bulb.

- Onions have a tendency to attract white rot and downy mildew, which are difficult to control. If you try your hand at onions and the bulbs do not produce as expected, the green shoots are a great secondary crop you can harvest instead.

- If you grow onions to store for winter use, you must dry them completely before storing or they will rot quickly.

- If there is rot on one onion in your storage bin it will spread to the others, ruining the entire bunch. Keeping a watchful eye on the onions in storage is necessary for successful winter storage.

Why gardeners like to grow this plant:
economy of growing in quantity for winter storage

- Onions are an interesting plant to grow, notwithstanding the difficulties with disease. You can grow a large quantity in a relatively small space and, in mass, the crop makes a pleasing sight.

- If properly dried and stored, onions make a great crop for winter storage.

Potatoes *(Solanaceae family)*

Why this plant is challenging:
significant labor required

- Potatoes grow as tubers and require a loose soil in order to form properly. In soils with a high clay content, the soil will need to be heavily amended with organic matter (compost) for proper crop growth. Note: a way around soil amending is to plant potatoes in containers with loose soil or in soil towers constructed of chicken wire.

- Because potatoes grow deep in the soil, the soil must be cultivated farther down than other root crops. Likewise in harvesting, potatoes must be dug deeply (and carefully) to harvest the entire crop. While not insurmountable, the labor required in both of these stages of the potato-growing cycle can be more than a new gardener is expecting, or willing to do.

Why gardeners like to grow this plant:
variety, winter-storage crop

- There are a number of wonderful heirloom varieties available that can be started from seed or seed potatoes.

- Potatoes do extremely well grown in containers.

- If properly dried and stored, potatoes make a great crop for winter storage.

Pumpkins, Jack-o'-lantern *(Cucurbita family)*

Why this plant is challenging:
season length, timing for Halloween use, early maintenance

- Pumpkins, Jack-o'-lantern and other varieties, take extra attention to establish; the young leaves attract slugs and need to be monitored in the early stages of growth.
- Pumpkins require a very long growing season, 120–150 days, depending upon the variety. If you are growing pumpkins for use as jack-o'-lanterns at Halloween, it is necessary to start the seeds inside as early as April so that they are ready for harvest in time for the holiday.

Why gardeners like to grow this plant:
fun, variety

- Watching the pumpkin plant grow is fun, sheer fun. Once established, it grows fast, takes up an enormous amount of space, and produces large, brightly colored fruit.
- There are a number of interesting varieties available to grow that are often not available in stores.

Strawberries *(Fragaria family)*

Why this plant is challenging:
disease prone, high maintenance

- Strawberries are prone to molds and tend to attract beetles, slugs, and birds; crop maintenance can be difficult.
- This plant is a perennial, reproducing by sending out runners. Strawberries can become invasive after only a few years.
- Once established, the strawberry patch must be thinned yearly of old plants to prevent both overcrowding and crop decline.
- Strawberries have a high water content and require consistent water throughout the spring and summer.
- While loving water, these plants do not like to sit on moist soil and they do not like to compete with weeds. This combination

of requirements means that gardeners have to mulch heavily. Mulching strawberries requires that each plant be carefully lifted up while mulch is placed underneath.

Why gardeners like to grow this plant:
taste, cost, challenge

- For those who love strawberries, there is nothing better than fresh berries picked from the garden. Strawberries can be very expensive to buy but quite inexpensive to grow, if you can provide the proper space and maintenance.

- Experienced gardeners love the challenge of growing strawberries.

Watermelons (*Citrullus family*)

Why this plant is challenging:
season length, high maintenance

- To produce sweet fruit, watermelons need a long growing season, which the lower Great Lakes region does not consistently provide. Planting from starts, and an acceptance of possible crop failure due to an early cold snap, are important for growing watermelons in our area. Note: there are varieties of short-season watermelons (for example, "Sweet Siberian") but it can be difficult to locate the seeds and they produce small, ball-shaped fruits, rather than the common large, oval-shaped fruit.

- Melons of all types need high levels of nutrients to develop successfully.

- Watermelons have a high water content and require consistent water throughout the spring and summer.

- Four-legged creatures seem to love to nibble on watermelons the moment they turn ripe. It can be frustrating to wait so long for a taste of ripe melon, only to find that something got there first.

Why gardeners like to grow this plant:
fun, variety, challenge

- Watermelons capture the imagination of children and are often grown to satisfy their curiosity.

- There are a number of rare and unusual varieties that can be grown from seed.

Epilogue

Gardening is an act of faith on many levels. We have faith the seeds we buy are viable. We have faith the spring will bring adequate amounts of sun and water, but not so much water that our garden drowns. We have faith that dogs, cats, deer, and other four-legged creatures find their food somewhere else, and not in our garden. And most importantly, we have faith that we will have the needed time and energy all season long to keep our garden in the best possible shape. By this faith that makes up a garden we become transformed; along the way we become gardeners.

Acknowledgements

~~~~~~

I am indebted to the Michigan Master Gardener Program, Ann Arbor's Discovery Garden community, and to the children of Haisley Elementary School's Garden Club for the endless educational and observational opportunities they collectively provided me over the last 15 years. A special thanks to Jill Peek for encouraging me to take on the task of writing this book, and for sticking with me to turn it into a reality.

— Sheri Repucci, Fall 2009

About the Author:

Sheri Repucci is an advanced master gardener who has been growing vegetables and perennials organically in the Great Lakes region since childhood. She's an active volunteer in her gardening community, where she has taught children the joys of gardening in small spaces for more than a dozen years. At Project Grow, Ann Arbor, Michigan's community gardening organization, she managed a program devoted to developing and continuing a lifelong love of gardening in seniors, children, and those with vision and other physical challenges. An expert on container gardening, Sheri is sought after as a speaker on growing vegetables organically in containers and raised beds.

Contributors:

KIM BAYER is a food writer and culinary researcher with a degree in Information and Library Science from the University of Michigan. She leads the local chapter of Slow Food and works with several other non-profit initiatives concerned with community food security. Kim's blog is called The Farmer's Marketer: http://thefarmersmarketer.com.

MELANIE BOYLE   is an artist and illustrator who finds inspiration in her own garden and in the dynamic graphic space of folk paper cutting traditions. A native of Vancouver, British Columbia, Canada, she now lives and works in Ann Arbor, Michigan, where she runs her studio, Cleverlotus Design.

ANNETTE SIFFIN   is a freelance graphic artist for print and web. She lives in Manchester, Michigan.

Resources

~~~~~~

Extension Services in the Lower Great Lakes

ILLINOIS

Extension Services:
http://web.extension.uiuc.edu/state/index.html
Office of Extension and Outreach
214 Mumford Hall (MC-710),
1301 W. Gregory Drive
Urbana, IL 61801
Phone: (217) 333-5900

Master Gardener Program:
http://web.extension.uiuc.edu/mg/
Department of Natural Resources and Environmental Sciences
1007 Plant Sciences Lab
1201 S. Dorner Drive MC-634
Urbana, IL 61801
Phone: (217) 265-5256

INDIANA

Extension Services:
www.ag.purdue.edu/extension/pages/default.aspx
Purdue Extension, Agricultural Administration Building
615 West State Street
West Lafayette, IN 47907-2053
Phone: (765) 494-8491

Master Gardener Program:
www.hort.purdue.edu/MG/
Purdue University
Department of Horticulture and Landscape Architecture
625 Agriculture Mall Drive
West Lafayette, IN 47907-2010
Phone: (765) 494-1296

MICHIGAN

Extension Services:
www.msue.msu.edu/portal/
Michigan State University Extension
Agriculture Hall, Room 108
Michigan State University
East Lansing, MI 48824-1039
Phone: (517) 355-2308

Master Gardener Program:
http://web1.msue.msu.edu/mastergardener/
1-888-MSUE-4MI
Phone: (888) 678-3464

NEW YORK

Extension Services:
www.cce.cornell.edu/

Master Gardener Program:
www.gardening.cornell.edu/education/mgprogram/
Department of Horticulture
Plant Science Building
Cornell University
Ithaca, NY 14853
Phone: (607) 255-5918

OHIO

Extension Services:
www.extension.osu.edu/
2120 Fyffe Road, Room 3
Ag Administration Building
Columbus, OH 43210
Phone: (614) 292-6181

Master Gardener Program:
www.hcs.ohio-state.edu/mg/
4400 Gateway Blvd. Suite 104
Springfield, OH 45502
Phone: (937) 328-4607

ONTARIO

Master Gardener Program:
www.mgoi.ca/

PENNSYLVANIA

Extension Services:
www.extension.psu.edu/
323 Ag Administration Building
University Park, PA 16802
Phone: (814) 865-4028

Master Gardener Program:
www.horticulture.psu.edu/extension/mg
2120 Cornwall Road, Suite 1
Lebanon PA 17042
Phone: (814) 404-8237

WISCONSIN

Extension Services:
www.uwex.edu/CES/

Master Gardener Program:
www.hort.wisc.edu/mastergardener/
Department of Horticulture
1575 Linden Drive
University of Wisconsin – Madison
Madison, WI 53706

Suggested Reading

FOOD GARDENING

C. E. Voigt and J. S. Vandemark, *Vegetable Gardening in the Midwest*
Cooperative Extension Service, College of Agriculture
University of Illinois, Urbana-Champaign, IL 2002

Jeanne Mackin, *The Cornell Book of Herbs & Edible Flowers*
Cornell Cooperative Extension, Ithaca, NY 1993

Lucy Peel, *Kitchen Garden: What to Grow and How to Grow It*
Harper Collins Publishers, New York, NY 2004

Rosalind Creasy, *The Edible Rainbow Garden,* Periplus Editions Ltd.
Boston, MA 2000

Yvonne Cuthbertson, *Success With Organic Vegetables*
Guild of Master Craftsmen Publications, Ltd., East Sussex, England 2006

Organic and General Gardening References

Emily Young and Dave Egbert, *Big Ideas for Small Gardens: Featuring Dave Egbert's Garden Notebook,* Sunset Books, Inc., Menlo Park, CA 2007

Fern Marshall Bradley and Barbara W. Ellis, *Rodale's All-New Encyclopedia of Organic Gardening: The Indispensable Resource for Every Gardener*
Rodale Press, Emmaus, PA 1992

Sunset Books and Sunset Magazine, *National Garden Book*
Sunset Books, Inc., Menlo Park, CA 1997

Container Gardening

Rose Marie Nichols McGee and Maggie Stuckey, *The Bountiful Container*
Workman Publishing, New York, NY 2002

Cooking

Bert Greene, *Greene on Greens,* Workman Publishing, New York, NY 1984

Janet Ballantyne, *Garden Way's Joy of Gardening Cookbook*
Storey Communications, Inc., Pownal, VT 1994

Seed Sources

Fedco Seeds
P. O. Box 520
Waterville, ME 04903
Phone: (207) 873-7333
www.fedcoseeds.com

Johnny's Selected Seeds
955 Benton Avenue
Winslow, ME 04901
Phone: (877) 564-6697
www.johnnyseeds.com

Index